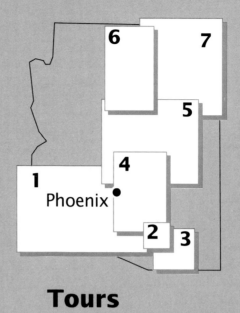

6

7

5

4

1

Phoenix

2

3

Tours

OTHER BOOKS BY TRAILER LIFE

An RVer's Annual: The Best of Trailer Life and Motorhome
Edited by Rena Copperman

This collector's edition of the best travel, technical, personality, and feature articles from past issues of the magazines, acknowledged as the leading publications in the RV field, is topped off with a special "Constitution" feature, recalling the recent nationwide anniversary celebration in prose and pictures. Beautiful four-color photos throughout . . . a great gift idea.
8½×11, 208 pages
$15.95 ISBN: 0-934798-21-4

Full-time RVing: A Complete Guide to Life on the Open Road
Bill and Jan Moeller

The answers to all the questions anyone who dreams of traveling full time in an RV may have can be found in this remarkable new source book. *Full-time RVing* takes the mystery out of fulltiming and makes it possible to fully enjoy this once-in-a-lifetime experience.
7¼×9¼, 352 pages
$14.95 ISBN: 0-934798-14-1

RX for RV Performance & Mileage
John Geraghty and Bill Estes

In 32 chapters, this book covers everything an owner must know about how an engine (particularly a V-8) works, vehicle maintenance, propane and diesel as alternative fuels, eliminating engine "ping," improving exhaust systems and fuel economy, and much more.
7¾×9¼, 359 pages
$14.95 ISBN: 0-934798-08-0

The Good Sam RV Cookbook
Edited by Beverly Edwards and the editors of *Trailer Life*

Over 250 easy and delicious recipes, including 78 prize-winners from Good Sam Samboree cook-offs around the country. Also contains tips, ideas, and suggestions to help you get the most from your RV galley.
7¼×9¼, 252 pages
$14.95 ISBN: 0-934798-17-6

These books are available at fine bookstores everywhere. Or, you may order directly from Trailer Life. For each book ordered, simply send us the name of the book, the price, plus $2 per book for shipping and handling (California residents please add 6½% sales tax). Mail to:

Trailer Life Books, P.O. Box 4500, Agoura, CA 91301

You may call our Customer Service representatives if you wish to charge your order or if you want more information. Please phone, toll-free, Monday through Friday, 7:00 A.M. to 6:00 P.M.; Saturday, 7:30 A.M. to 12:30 P.M. Pacific Time, **1-800-234-3450.**

RVing America's Backroads:

Arizona

Kitty Pearson
and
Jim Vincent

…Light-hearted I take to the open road,
Healthy, free, the world before me,
The long brown path before me leading
wherever I choose.

Walt Whitman, *Song of the Open Road*

Trailer Life Books
Agoura, California

DEDICATION
This book is dedicated with gratitude to our parents

Trailer Life Book Division

President: Richard Rouse
Vice President/General Manager: Ted Binder
Vice President/Publisher, Book Division: Michael Schneider
General Manager, Book Division: Rena Copperman
Assistant Manager, Book Division: Cindy Lang

Cover design: Bob Schroeder
Interior design: David Fuller/Robert S. Tinnon
Production manager: Rena Copperman
Production coordinator: Robert S. Tinnon
Editorial assistants: Judi Lazarus and Martha Weiler
Indexer: Barbara Wurf
Maps: EarthSurface Graphics
Color separations: Western Laser Graphics, Inc.

All photographs are the authors' unless otherwise credited.
Cover photo by John W. Warden

Opinions expressed by the authors
are not necessarily those of the publisher.

This book was set in ITC Garamond Book by Andresen's Tucson
Typographics and printed on 60-pound Multiweb Gloss by
R.R. Donnelley and Sons in Willard, Ohio.

ISBN 0-934798-25-7

Library of Congress Cataloging-in-Publication Data

Pearson, Kitty, 1946–
    RVing America's backroads: Arizona / Kitty Pearson and Jim Vincent.
        p. cm.
    Includes index.
    ISBN 0-934798-25-7
    1. Automobile travel—Arizona—Guide-books.   2. Recreational
    vehicles—Arizona. 3. Arizona—Description and travel—1981— —
    Guide-books.   I. Vincent, Jim, 1949– .   II. Title.   III. Title:
    Arizona.
    GV1024.P24   1989   88-24785 CIP
    917.89—dc19

Contents

ACKNOWLEDGMENTS

Our travels were helped immeasurably by the moral support of our editor, Rena Copperman. Other good people who helped were Bob Livingston, archivist Sue Abbey at Prescott's Sharlot Hall Museum, and Fleetwood Enterprises, Inc. for our use of a Southwind motorhome.

Excerpts from *Helldorado* by William Breakenridge, Copyright 1928 by William M. Breakenridge. Copyright renewed 1956. Reprinted by permission of Houghton Mifflin Company.

Excerpt from *Sharlot Hall on the Arizona Strip: A Diary of a Journey Through Northern Arizona in 1911,* by Sharlot M. Hall, edited by C. Gregory Crampton, published by Northland Publishing. Copyright 1975. All rights reserved. Used with permission.

Brief excerpts from pages 7; 47; 184–85; 300; 308; 364–65; 391; 427 of Marshall Trimble's *Roadside History of Arizona,* published and copyright 1986 by Mountain Press Publishing Company, Missoula, Montana.

Preface

Before you lies an unparalleled adventure: a backroads tour of Arizona, the Grand Canyon State. Please join us, *or* let this book whet your appetite to take your own trip. Our routes are suggestions; you might devise your own. This is only a starting point in discovering that Arizona offers so much more besides the Grand Canyon.

One way to fire the imagination is to look at a map of the state. See "Meteor Crater" or "Arizona-Sonora Desert Museum"? Perhaps you'll say: "I want to see that!" That's what we did, and you can, too. You can see all the sights and learn more than you ever imagined possible. Backroad wandering is a state of mind, and Arizona exploration is a perfect place to heighten that state. We followed the roads as they opened before us, revealing sights, sounds, and people of the state. We avoided superhighways, by and large, and dallied only briefly in cities. Time spent in urban areas provided a historic and cultural background, deeply enriching our travels on "genuine" backroads.

Every effort has been made to build a reliable base of information in this volume, but we urge you to seek out local sources of information and to recheck routes, admission fees, and necessary reservations (Arizona is a favorite place for RVers year-round) where it seems advisable. This is simply prudent RVing.

The Golden Eagle Passport is invaluable for those traveling extensively to national parks and monuments. At present it costs $25 annually and can be bought directly at parks and monuments or by mail from the National Park Service, U.S. Department of the Interior, 18th and C streets N.W., Washington, D.C. 20240. The Golden Age Passport is free to permanent U.S. residents sixty-two or older. The Golden Access Passport is free to permanently blind or disabled travelers. The latter two must be applied for in person at most federally operated recreation areas that charge an entrance fee.

ARIZONA

Buddy Mays

Arizona has long been a golden land attracting travelers to its fantastic interior. Migrating Paleo-Indians, Spaniards, gold miners, and pioneers have all been a part of the state's panoramic history. The Grand Canyon State, with its natural and cultural riches, is a mother lode for travelers today in America's Southwest. Yet, the state seems protected by its cliffs and mountains, a bastion from encroachment. It's this sense of sanctuary, the inviolable rocky wilderness or the intractable desert fastness, that draws so many. The variety of sights can literally stagger the mind: the world's largest meteor crater, national monuments and parks (more than any other state), Spanish missions and presidios, fabled old western towns, immense reservation lands, endless recreational opportunities, and vibrant cities. It's no wonder then that Arizona ranks so highly with RVers as a wintering ground and a year-round destination spot.

We'd lived in and visited Arizona before we traveled its backroads, but familiarity with one section only showed us how different are its other parts. Each step of the journey deserves full concentration and curiosity. But there's no need to rush; the beauty of secondary roads is the luxury of time. Highways are for going places; backroads are for wandering. You'll find the people of the state as interesting a blend as the food of the region. Arizona is multicultural, with the nation's third-largest Native American population and a vital Hispanic community, as well as transplanted residents from every part of the country.

The cultural complexity, the scenic diversity and grandeur all provide a compelling motivation for exploring. With an area of 113,909 square miles (seventy percent of the land is government owned or controlled), there are lots of wild places to ramble. Some backroads here aren't for the large trailer or motorhome; there are even roads of no return, like the one to Zane Grey's cabin. Other routes are navigable and paved, and they lead the adventurous to such scenic masterpieces as Sedona, the Mogollon Rim, and the Apache Trail.

Following the map traced by backroads over Arizona's surface, you'll find contrasts from the towering San Francisco Mountains around Flagstaff to the vast Sonora Desert. There are backroad routes through the Petrified Forest and Monument Valley, over to the sights of thriving Tucson, and into the White Mountains. At every turn, change and discovery awaken the imagination. For those who've come before, the backroads are a new way to know Arizona; for the first-time visitor, there's an unforgettable odyssey ahead.

Opposite photo by Buddy Mays

WIDE OPEN SPACES

Sonoran Desert Explorations

*Fort Yuma is probably the hottest place on earth.
The thermometer stays at one hundred and twenty
in the shade there all the time—except when
it varies and goes higher. . . . There is a
tradition . . . that a very very wicked soldier died
there, once, and of course went straight to the
hottest corner of perdition—the next day he
telegraphed back for his blankets.*

Mark Twain,
Roughing It

Roger and Donna Aitkenhead

2

W e could feel our adventure beginning as we entered Arizona from the west on Interstate 10/US Highway 95. Exploring the state's backroads had been a lifelong dream, and we rolled into southern Arizona's famed Sonora Desert, ready for its many surprises.

Quartzsite

A few years ago, while traveling in British Columbia, we'd met a rock and gem collector, a fellow RVer, who said he always wintered in Quartzsite, Arizona. His stories of avid rock hounds piqued our curiosity about the collectors' mecca. Each year, thousands of RVers migrate to Quartzsite to prospect, trade, and camp free of charge in the desert.

While the town of Quartzsite has improved RV parks and campsites, the surrounding desert is one of the largest recreational vehicle rough-camping areas in the United States. As well as the inexpensive camping, many modern RV pioneers who pull their wagons into state desert areas (requiring completely self-contained camping) come for the annual gem and mineral show.

Starting on the first Wednesday of February and running through the weekend, Quartzsite's Gem and Mineral Pow Wow swells the town's summer population from 500 residents to an estimated 750,000 people! All are interested in buying or selling rocks, gems, and jewelry. Entertainment during the Pow Wow includes rock and gem cutting and polishing demonstrations, as well as exhibits, workshops, and a giant swap meet. For additional information, contact the Quartzsite Improvement Association, Box 881, Quartzsite 85346, (602) 927-6325.

Hi Jolly's Grave

After cruising around the rough campsites, we went to the cemetery at Quartzsite's north end to view a monument to the man who might have said, "I'd walk a mile for a camel," Hadji Ali. His name was converted to "Hi Jolly" by American solders and pioneers in a strange historic episode.

Unbelievable as it may seem now, in 1857 Lieutenant Edward F. "Ned" Beale used camels and dromedaries instead of mules as pack animals while plotting the course of a railroad along the thirty-fifth parallel. A camel was able to carry twice the load of a mule, feed on desert plants, and subsist on little water, but in order to wrangle the temperamental camels, drivers had to be brought from the Middle East. The most re-nowned of these was Hi Jolly.

It seems that some of the animals were turned loose with the hope of perpetuating a camel herd, but the experiment failed, partly because the sight of them caused horses, mules, and cattle to stampede, an ironic twist in a land where camels once thrived in a prehistoric age.

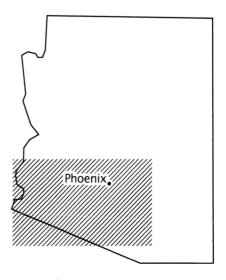

Tour 1 420 miles

QUARTZSITE • KOFA NATIONAL WILDLIFE REFUGE • YUMA • PAINTED ROCKS STATE PARK • GILA BEND • AJO • WHY • ORGAN PIPE NATIONAL MONUMENT • TOHONO O'ODHAM INDIAN RESERVATION • KITT PEAK OBSERVATORY

Sunset.
In the skies over Arizona's deserts, the sunsets are painted with clarity and brilliance. This moment of grandeur appeared at day's end in the Organ Pipe Cactus National Monument.

Walk a Mile for a Camel.
The gravesite of Hadji Ali, camel driver and scout famed in the area of Quartzsite, is a famous spot to visit.

While the other camel drivers returned to the Middle East, Hi Jolly stayed around Quartzsite until his death. He was memorialized by the stone pyramid over his grave. We stopped to photograph the unusual monument, marveling over the remembrances of him and other unlikely characters who have contributed to our country. Later, as we topped off our gas tanks at a filling station, we found it amusing that a mechanic was humming the folk song, "Hi Jolly," written by Randy Sparks (and performed by the New Christy Minstrels in the 1960s), that had set Hi Jolly's story to music.

Bruce Leonard, Jr.

The Lure of the Lode.
Nothing can quite describe the fever that accompanies a gathering of rock hounds when collectors and prospectors share the lore and their love of geology.

The Lure of Gold

As we sped south on US 95 toward the Kofa Wildlife Refuge, we fantasized about the gold story a Quartzsite resident had related. (Perhaps such tales are another reason why so many RVers flock to the area.) In 1884, a man nicknamed P. J. Perkins was superintendent for the Planet Mines (it was on the Bill Williams River, northeast of Quartzsite). Perkins had the experience all gold miners dream about on the way back from Tyson's Wells. Waylaid by a sandstorm, he was saved temporarily by some sheltering rocks while the storm raged on. Finally, the weather becalmed, and behind him was an exposed mother lode: a giant vein of gold ore. He took some pieces with him but staked the spot with his six-shooter and overcoat. Then he began a northward trek toward home, but his luck ran out in the desert, his riderless horse evidence of his death. A search party found his body half-covered with sand, but before he died, Perkins had scrawled these words in a notebook: "Found gold ledge by rocks fifteen feet high. Two rocks alike. Knocked off some pieces. Very rich. Dust in air too thick to tell exact location. Think it is above ravine I come up 7 miles." He would have been a rich man; the gold carried in his holster was assayed at $25,000 per ton.

No one to this date has ever found the site of the virgin ore known as the Lost Six-Shooter Mine, but it lies somewhere near Milepost 69 between Quartzsite and the Yuma County line. Perhaps some enterprising RV prospector will find it while wintering in Quartzsite.

Quartzsite was originally named Tyson's Wells for Charles Tyson who found water there in 1856. Tyson's Wells became a stage station on the road from Ehrenberg to Prescott, a fort for defense against hostile Mojave Indians.

Buddy Mays

King of Kofa.
The desert bighorn sheep is monarch of the Kofa National Wildlife Refuge. While many species in the Sonoran Desert region are endangered or threatened, at Kofa these handsome animals have a haven. Extremely agile, the bighorn can jump twenty vertical feet down rocky cliffs.

Kofa National Wildlife Refuge

Our continued travels brought us just south of the Yuma county line. To the east of US 95 lies the Kofa Wildlife Refuge, named for the King of Arizona Mining Company, whose property was stamped with "K of A." This mining operation, which produced $3,500,000 in gold between 1896 and 1910, is located southwest in the Kofa Range. We went to the mine by taking the dirt road at Stone Cabin (once a stage stop on the road between Ehrenberg and Yuma), then continuing about another twenty-two miles on a good washboard gravel road.

There are two other gravel roads into the Kofa refuge. One of the more popular goes to Palm Canyon; another is the Crystal Hill Road. Arizona's only native palm trees grow in Palm Canyon, nine miles north and east of Stone Cabin. A towering species of palm trees called *Washingtonia filifera* can be seen after a half hour's hike in a stunning red-rock-and-wildflower-lined canyon. If you're lucky, you may also view some rare, elusive desert bighorn sheep in the refuge.

Kofa Lore

We've spent a lot of time in the "bush" and have found that life in the outback either drives you crazy or gives you a sense of humor. Soldiers in the 1860s jokingly referred to the Kofa range as the "S.H. Mountains" because the appearance of certain peaks bore a similarity to large buildings with outhouses behind them. Curious ladies asking the meaning of S.H. were given a more delicate translation—"Short Horn."

Yuma—Penitentiary Bound

Yuma was our next stop; we headed directly for the Territorial Prison State Park, depicted so graphically in film, television, and literary works, and symbolizing the harsh penitentiary conditions between 1876 and 1909. The thought of ever being imprisoned in such a place has always seemed horrifying, yet Yuma was actually considered a model prison in its time, punishment being limited to the ball and chain for those attempting to escape. There was a prison hospital, a doctor, even a school for convicts who wanted to learn to read and write, and one of the first free public libraries in the territory; books were bought with funds collected by a twenty-five-cent charge to visitors.

Memorabilia from the Prison's Past

On display in the museum are photographs of past inmates and wardens, including a warden's wife who foiled a prison break by firing a Gatling gun at the would-be escapees. Among these historic photographs are images of Mormon polygamists who endured a term at Yuma, several people incarcerated for adultery, as well as convicts who perpetrated other crimes against nature and society. Grand larceny topped the list of wrongdoings.

Iron-Bar Hotel.
Stepping inside Yuma's territorial prison, the sense of confinement is claustrophobic. One of the prison's dungeons was known as the "snake pit." Cells were lined with iron bands to prevent prisoners from digging out to freedom.

Pearl Hart achieved great notoriety in 1899 as the infamous "girl bandit." She and her boyfriend, Joe Boot, held up a stagecoach north of Florence, but were caught and brought to justice in Yuma. Pearl was a natural actress and played to the court with her feminine wiles. The jury responded and freed her, incensing the judge, who again charged her for absconding with the stagedriver's revolver. Now here was a charge to which the jury could relate. Pearl "got time" in the Yuma Territorial Prison, while her boyfriend, Joe, hightailed it out of town, gone forever. Yet, Pearl's name went up in lights; she was famous. After getting out of Yuma Prison, Pearl did a stint in show business, but finally married a cowboy and led a quiet life in Globe, Arizona.

Yuma's Arts and Crafts

The highlights of the museum are the wonderful handicraft exhibits of the prisoners' work. There's a reproduction of a painting of Jesus done by an Austrian prisoner; the eyes appear to open and close if viewed from a certain angle. Other exhibits feature delightfully delicate lacework made by both men and women, as well as remarkably fine braided horsehair hatbands. The convicts had time on their hands and created outstandingly intricate detail reminiscent of the art of marlinespike done on whaling ships in the 1800s.

Life in Prison

Surprisingly, the cells, made from metal and masonry, are actually quite cool; still we could easily imagine that during the heat of summer's 120° days, the tiny spaces would be a living hell and we had no desire to linger in this "iron-bar hotel."

Tuberculosis was prevalent in the territory and along with other diseases took the lives of 113 inmates. Eight were shot while trying to escape, but 26 went over the wall to freedom. A total of 3,069 convicts, including 29 women, were confined at Yuma during its thirty years of operation.

As we traveled east, leaving Yuma on I-8, we heeded warnings on the Arizona map and were careful not to wander from the route because the Barry M. Goldwater Air Force Range lies to the south and the Yuma Proving Ground to the north. We had no choice but to take the interstate; there are no legal backroads in this national defense area.

Painted Rocks State Park

Our route took us to Painted Rocks State Park. From exit 102 off I-8, it's fourteen miles west of Gila Bend, then eleven miles north on Painted Rocks Road to Painted Rocks State Park. The park protects a national heritage of native petroglyphs and rock carvings depicting many images including human figures, snakes, and birds.

The Southwest is an outdoor art gallery of pictographs (rock paintings), and petroglyphs (rock carvings). Intense sunlight produces a dark-brown chemical patina on the smooth faces of basaltic rocks. When the patina is penetrated by a sharp tool or a pounding stone, a lighter-colored layer is revealed and may remain visible for centuries.

Origins of the Petroglyphs

Painted Rocks may have been the natural boundary marker separating lands claimed by two divisions of the ancient Hohokam people, perhaps the ancestors of the present day Maricopa Indians to the east and the Quechans, or Yumas, to the west. We discovered several schools of thought on the makers of petroglyphs. One suggests they were the result of idle doodling by sentries, lookouts, or laborers (possibly women) bored after long hours of tilling fields and gathering seeds and roots.

Arizona State Parks Staff, Cheryl Steenerson

Prehistoric Artisans.
Were these images the reason Father Kino called the place the Painted Mountains? The petroglyphs tell stories without words, and we could only guess at the missing chapters.

Another theory suggests that petroglyphs have a more religious, ritualistic, cabalistic, or even astronomic meaning (the Lascaux cave murals in France were the ultimate neolithic pictographs and obviously had a deeply ritualistic significance), and a third theory holds that the petroglyphs were the newspapers of the day, telling others where the carvers had been and what game was in the area.

It's a mystery, and scientists are divided on the true intent of petroglyphs and pictographs. Only the vanished people who created them could have enlightened us as to their true meanings.

RV Parks

There is a small RV campground with room for about twenty-five vehicles in Painted Rocks State Historic Park, but because of the lack of water it's more convenient for completely self-contained vehicles. Another state campground is located a mile north of the historic park on the same access road. It has thirty-seven sites, with table-bench units and fire pits, and ten have ramadas (arbors) for shade. Both charge a fee, but the second one has drinking water, restrooms, hot showers, and a dump station. There is also a small lake that has largemouth bass, crappie, and some enormous carp, although the Arizona Department of Health recom-

It Was a Hoot.
Bubo virginianus, the Great Horned Owl, can be found throughout Arizona. Here, a young owl naps in the bright daylight hours.

New Friends.
An Arizona farm boy from Gila Bend and his pet goat make a nice image of life in backroad country.

mends that the fish not be eaten because of pollution. During the winter, a variety of migratory water fowl, including flocks of sea gulls, use the impoundment.

Gila Bend

We spent the night at the latter campground; next morning we packed up the motorhome and continued east on I-8 to Gila Bend. There are rich layers of history here, a virtual procession of inhabitants and visitors. In 1774, Franciscan Padre Francisco Garces reported a Papago *rancheria* at Gila Bend, which he named *Santos Apostales San Simon y Judas.* There are vestiges of the Butterfield Stage stations along the Gila River, as well as Fortaleza, an ancient fortified hill that can be seen four miles northwest of the town. The Gatlin site, an important archaeological dig, is situated several miles to the north. It's a relic of the Hohokam people who've been traced to the Gila River area as early as the third century B.C. Archaeologists generally agree that the Hohokam migrated north from Mexico or Central America, their culture evolving over one to two thousand years; the partly excavated Gatlin site is one of the westernmost settlements.

Stagecoach Days

The location of the Butterfield Overland Mail Station established in 1858 is about four miles from present-day Gila Bend. Indians burned it in 1860, but that didn't deter the operation for long. Gila Ranch was one of the timetable stations (like Tucson and Yuma), each stop separated by fifteen to twenty miles. The first history-making journey began at 6:00 P.M. on the evening of September 16, 1858, at Tipton, Missouri, 160 miles west of St. Louis, ending in San Francisco, California, 23 days and 23½ hours later. We imagined the stage driver blowing a bugle two miles out of each way station to alert the wranglers to ready a fresh team of horses. Upon arrival of the stage, letters were exchanged while passengers headed for the outhouses. Within ten minutes the stage was on the trail again. We read the journal of William Tallack, a passenger on the Butterfield Stage traveling east; meals at the way station were a little different in 1860 than at a modern truck stop.

> We took our next meal at 2 P.M. at Gila Bend. This station had been destroyed by the Indians only four months previously, but the inmates escaped. More than a hundred arrows were afterwards picked up around the spot. . . .
>
> The fare, though rough, is better than could be expected so far from civilized districts and consists of bread, tea, and fried steaks of bacon, venison, antelope, or mule flesh—the latter tough enough.

Ajo

We turned south on Arizona State Route 85, which brought us to the copper-and-silver-mining town of Ajo. At first, we thought Ajo, meaning garlic in Spanish, was named after the pungent seasoning. The town really

At Day's End.
This church in Ajo is a classic piece of architecture. Father Kino and the Jesuits generally respected the Papago beliefs, and the two religions were meshed within the Sonoran Catholic Church, still a strong force in the area.

got its name from *Au'auho*, the Papago word for paint (the red-ore pigment was employed by Papagos to decorate their skin). With a lovely white church at its center, Ajo has a history as one of Arizona's richest copper camps, which peaked during World War I. In 1917, when old Ajo burned down, the citizens were tired of living in Cornelia Copper's company town. A man named Sam Clark took the situation in hand and planned a new village. And the place prospered; there were 1,000 citizens in 1917. When the copper company prepared its revenge, refusing to sell the people water, citizens, with typical American ingenuity, used an old mine shaft as the site of their well. One interesting tombstone at the local cemetery is completely written in copper wire.

Why Why?

Continuing south on SR 85 we came to the town of Why. We asked a resident why the town is called *Why*; the answer? It's situated on a junction, or "Y," in the road. To the north, SR 85 goes to Ajo; southward, it leads to the American border town of Lukeville. Tucson is east on SR 86.

Robert J. Smith

The Southern Empire.
The Sonoran Desert region lies in Arizona and in the Mexican states of Sonora and the two Bajas. This area includes not only desert, but subtropical swamps, deciduous woodlands, prairies, coldwater streams and pools, alpine meadows, and crags.

After this explanation, we asked another resident why she chose to live here, and she replied, "Why not?" In 1970, the independent citizens of Why established an RV park. (**Note**: Had we been heading over the southern border, we could have purchased Mexican Traveler's Insurance here for the trip down Mexico's Highway 2 or 8.)

Beautiful Desert Environs

Lining SR 85 south are ocotillo, with their beautiful red flowers, and giant saguaro cacti. Teddybear cholla, that furry, beautiful, yet nasty cactus, also known as "jumping" cactus for those who brush near it, is prevalent, and hikers should be wary. The spines of this fuzzy plant will stick to flesh or clothing, and we were especially watchful of our dog, Winston, since he was unfamiliar with the hazards of the desert and particularly the jumping cactus. The best remedy, by the way, for dog or human is a pair of pliers and tweezers.

The Ocotillo.
Pronounced o-ko-<u>tee</u>-yo, this common, funnel-shaped plant grows on open, stoney slopes in the desert. Clusters of red flowers appear from March through June.

Robert J. Smith

Roger and Donna Aitkenhead

Buddy Mays

An Array of Succulents.
This array of cacti includes *(opposite)* the organ pipe, *(top)* the senita, the saguaro *(left)*, and the fishhook *(above)*. Each has adapted in its way to the rigorous demands of life in the desert.

Organ Pipe Cactus National Monument

From Why we drove south on SR 85 into the Organ Pipe Cactus National Monument, some 516 square miles of untouched desert dedicated to a rare succulent. The dimensions of the monument are about half the size of Rhode Island, and there are two dirt roads from the information center, about twenty-two miles from Why. One road is twenty-one miles long, the other is thirty-five. The Park Service does not allow you to tow a trailer on these roads, nor is it advisable for motorhomes longer than twenty-five feet to venture over the one-way, bouncy washboard routes. Visitors can unhook either the tow or towed vehicle, leaving the trailer or motorhome at the monument's spacious campground (where recreational vehicles over twenty-eight feet long must park in designated blue spaces).

Backroads of the Monument

We found the dirt-road tours worth the time. The Ajo Mountain Drive weaves from the floor of the Sonora Desert through the edges of the Ajo Range and then into the Sonoita Valley. As we climbed gradually, we saw a variety of beautiful cacti in the red-rock canyons and organ pipe cacti

RVing Organ Pipe.
The wide open spaces of Organ Pipe Cactus National Monument contain an area larger than the Great Smoky Mountains National Park of North Carolina and Tennessee. RVers can wander many miles through this prickly kingdom, as did Father Kino when he pioneered a route known as *El Camino del Diablo* (The Devil's Highway) between Sonoita, Mexico, and the area of today's Yuma. Gold prospectors also crossed the future monument's grounds between 1849 and 1860.

Roger and Donna Aitkenhead

Roger and Donna Aitkenhead

Verdant Oasis.
Quitobaquito Springs is the reward for traveling part of the longer monument-loop-road known as Puerto Blanco Drive. The route circles around the Puerto Blanco Mountains, down near the Mexican border, and finally back to State Route 85.

growing on the hillsides. The organ pipe is not unlike the saguaro, which has arms growing from a central trunk. With the organ pipe cactus there is a profusion of trunks, eighteen to twenty feet in height.

The longer one-way route passes Quitobaquito Springs, and there are side canyons off this route that lead to vistas of the other rare cactus, the senita. It resembles the organ pipe but has fewer ribs and at its tip, whiskery spines resembling Grandpa's beard. There are 29 types of cacti and 250 species of birds here, but our favorite is the melodic Gambel's quail rooster. March or April is the time for flower lovers to visit the monument; with a wet winter, the desert presents a glorious array of blossoms.

Tohono O'Odham (Papago) Indian Reservation

If we'd driven south on SR 85 we could have entered Mexico at Lukeville, (border closed from midnight to 8:00 A.M.), but we turned around and went north back to the junction at Why, driving east on SR 86 to the Tohono O'Odham (Papago) Indian Reservation. The words *Tohono O'Odham* (pronounced Tohono O-Otam) mean "People of the Desert," and the reservation is huge (with an area of 2.8 million acres), topped in size only by the Navajo domain. This world is one of timelessness. Many anthropologists believe the Papago were closely related to the powerful Aztec Indians of central Mexico. Even today, many words used in their language and prayers are considered Uto-Aztecan.

Some History of a People

In 1687, Father Eusebio Kino began his missionary work with the O'Odham people. Until then, the Indian diet had consisted of jackrabbit, deer, quail, and the mesquite beans they gathered (one interpretation of the word *Papago* is from the Pima Indian language meaning "bean eater"). They also dug roots and picked the fruit of the saguaro, cholla, prickly pear, and barrel cacti. During the summer they grew crops of melon, squash, maize and cotton; the Spaniards' important contribution to their diet was winter wheat and barley.

The O'Odham Indians were peaceful. While Apache raiders made warfare a way of life, the O'Odham were usually aggressive only for defensive reasons, as in the late 1700s when Apaches intermittently invaded O'Odham lands, raiding for horses, women, children, and food. When finally provoked, the O'Odham were fierce warriors and fought courageously. Once having slain an enemy, custom dictated that a Papago warrior quit fighting and blacken his face at the rear of the battle. He and his wife were thought to be corrupted by the killing; a sixteen-day fast was necessary to cleanse them.

Both the Pima and Papago had amicable relations with Anglos. In fact, the O'Odham never fought against the United States; still, they had no protective treaty against infringement by Anglo society. Although the reservation was given to them in 1906, the mineral rights weren't theirs until 1959. And only in 1949 did they get the right to vote (the last reservation).

The Art of Craftsmanship

We drove east on SR 86 through the tribal towns of Quijotoa and Sells. We chatted with friendly Indian women at the trading posts; they were selling artifacts, jewelry, and handwoven baskets while children scurried happily about. These people seem at peace, cheerful about their lives. One place we missed, but heard about later, was a church in the village of Pisinimo (south on Indian Route 21 from SR 86). This unique church has designs by Frank Mariano, a gifted O'Odham, and a mural by David Sine, an Apache artist.

The O'Odham are famous for their beautifully crafted coiled baskets. The intestines or warp of the baskets are created from bear grass (*Nolina micocarpa*), which looks like the urban pampas grass. The weft, or the material that is wrapped around the warp, is yucca (*Yucca elata*) that's been left in the sun to bleach to a bright white, while Devil's Claw (*Martynia parviflora*), another weft material, is used for the black designs in the baskets.

After all the materials are gathered and prepared, the weaving begins. The yucca and Devil's Claw are wrapped around the finely split bear grass, and slowly the coils are joined by punching a hole in the lower coil with an awl, then inserting the weft material through that hole and pulling it tight over the higher coil, thus literally sewing the basket together. The baskets are tight enough to hold water or saguaro cactus wine, the fruit of the saguaro made into wine and used in a spring fertility custom.

Tribal Myth

One recurrent basket motif is the "Man in the Maze," which tells a Creation myth not unlike a combination of Noah and Theseus and the Minotaur. It concerns a flood that wiped out a corrupt people, and how I'itoi, "the elder brother," was allowed by the Creator to watch the disaster. I'itoi was instrumental in creating the Hohokam people from whom Papago and Pima peoples descended, but he was eventually killed by ignorant people, his spirit returning to Baboquivari Peak. The tribespeople believe the deity still calls the mountain home.

The other aspect of the Man in the Maze is a more universal idea of evolution through life, the maze tightening as the life traveler comes ever nearer to the center, death, and God. Near life's end, the individual has a time to reflect, to find an inner peace before reaching the center. The origin of the design is a mystery, except that the identical form has been discovered on the island of Crete in the Mediterranean. Also, inside one of the inner rooms at Casa Grande near Phoenix, the form of the maze was scratched into the caliche material of a wall, an unsolved enigma in the spiritual life of an ancient culture. We stopped at the church in Quijotoa, which has colorful windows depicting the maze design with the figure of a man directly above the path's beginning. Mysteries like these drew us ever deeper into the fascinating story of Arizona's history. The myth of the maze brought to mind our own odyssey on the backroads of Arizona. At every twist and turn in the road there was a new discovery and another challenge.

Driving in the Desert

As we left Sells, a light rain started to fall. We drove east on SR 86 across the reservation, admiring the pastel colors of the green and yellow Palo Verde trees, interspersed with the radiant red flowers of ocotillo and purple fruit topping saguaro cacti. Though it was warm and humid, we turned off the air conditioner and drove with the windows down. The sweet, almost pinelike, smell of the desert known as "desert perfume" filled the motorhome. We took huge gulps of air, savoring the perfume, joking that a fortune could be made by anyone bottling this olfactory delicacy.

The Heights of Kitt Peak

At the junction with SR 386, we turned south and began the climb to Kitt Peak, 6,875 feet high in the Quinlan Mountains. Baboquivari Peak, at 7,730 feet the highest in the area, is the Tohono O'Odham people's sacred

The Heard Museum

A Fascinating Enigma.
The mystery of life is portrayed symbolically in the "Man in the Maze" design. This powerful image may have been carried over by early Spaniards or developed by ancestors of the Pimas and Papagos. Nothing yet explains the presence of the identical motif on some coins of ancient Crete.

Buddy Mays

The Sun and the Stars.
In 1893, Kitt Peak may have been named for Kit, an Indian cook and errand boy for a local surveying team. Or the married name of a crew member's sister may have been the source. Such were the humble origins for the name of one of the largest concentration of solar and stellar research facilities, founded in 1958.

mountain, where their deity, I'itoi, lives. In negotiations for the use of Kitt Peak for astronomical observation, it was agreed that the mountain's caves would be left untouched by the government in order to assure that I'itoi, in his sometime form of a coyote, would have a place to seek refuge.

A national observatory, Kitt Peak was chosen for its clear desert air, as far as possible from city lights. One of the National Optical Astronomy Observatories (NOAO), it's run by the Association of Universities for Research in Astronomy, in which seventeen universities work cooperatively under the auspices of the National Science Foundation. Astronomers from around the world come to work at this facility that houses twenty-two telescopes, among them the McMath solar telescope, the largest of its kind, used for studying the sun. We admired the massive Mayall four-meter telescope, which is nineteen stories high, the nation's second-largest reflector. This $10-million telescope weighs 375 tons, yet is balanced so perfectly that surveys of the stars are accomplished with a one-half-horsepower motor.

Caution is advised when visiting Kitt Peak on a wet day in winter, where desert rain can turn to mountain snow, icing the roads. Call ahead if you want to be safe ([602] 620-5350).

POINTS OF INTEREST: Arizona Tour 1

Sonoran Desert Explorations

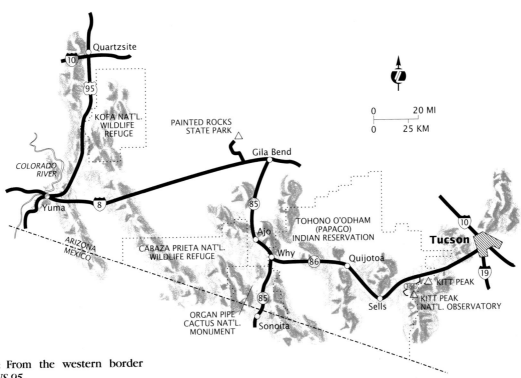

ACCESS: From the western border on *I-10/US 95.*

INFORMATION: *Quartzsite Improvement Association*, Box 881, Quartzsite 85346 (602) 927-6325; *Yuma County Chamber of Commerce*, 377 Main St., Yuma 85364, or P.O. Box 230, Yuma 85366; (602) 782-2567.

ANNUAL EVENTS:

Quartzsite: *Annual Gem and Mineral Pow Wow*, first weekend in February.

Yuma: *San Diego Padres* play baseball at the Desert Sun Stadium during spring training January–March, (602) 782-2567; *horse racing* at Yuma County Fair Grounds, last two weekends October, first two weekends November, (602) 726-4420; *Greyhound Park*, October 31–April 9, (602) 726-4655; *Arizona Historical Society Century House Museum*, historical building at 240 S. Madison, Tuesday–Saturday 10 A.M.–4 P.M.,

Sunday noon–4 P.M. (October–April); *Quechan Indian Museum*, Indian Hill Rd., old military post, Monday–Friday 8 A.M.–noon and 1–5 P.M.; *Yuma Territorial State Prison*, Giss Pkwy and Prison Hill Rd., daily 8 A.M.–5 P.M.; *Yuma Art Center*, 281 Gila St., (602) 783-2314.

NEARBY ATTRACTIONS:

Kitt Peak: *National Optical Astronomy Observatory*, NOAO Public Information Office, Box 26732, Tucson 85726-6732 (602) 327-5511.

Buddy Mays

GEM IN THE DESERT
The Tucson Area

On the . . . east . . . the . . . massive outlines of
the Santa Rita peak overshadowing the town
of Tucson, and the white, glaring roof of the
beautiful mission ruin of San Xavier del Bac . . .
one of the most beautiful and picturesque edifices
of the kind to be found on the North American
continent. I was surprised to see such a splendid
monument of civilization in the wilds of Arizona.

J. Ross Browne,
Adventures in the Apache Country

T ucson is so vibrant in its color-washed landscape of mountains and deserts, we always feel glad to be there. This remarkable city graciously embraces past and present in one of the handsomest parts of Arizona. The name *Tucson* comes from the Pima Indian word *schookson*, meaning "black at the foot," a reference to the dark base of the nearby Sentinel Mountains.

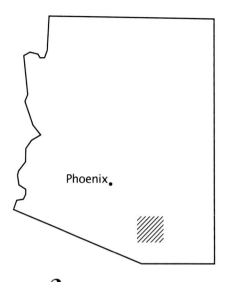

Tour **2** *100 miles*

TUCSON • SAGUARO NATIONAL MONUMENT • SABINO CANYON • MOUNT LEMMON • SAN XAVIER DEL BAC • GREEN VALLEY

Tucson's Early Days

The area's first real European was the padre on horseback, Eusebio Francisco Kino, a Jesuit priest. He came in November, 1694, establishing a mission station or *visita* in the wilderness called *San Augustin de Oiaur*, that would later become Tucson. After several attempts to build a mission were thwarted by raiding Apaches, the *visita* hung on, allied with its parent mission, San Xavier del Bac. By 1775, Spain became more aggressive with Apache raiders; on August 20 of that year a red-headed Irish mercenary named Colonel Hugo O'Connor, accompanied by Father Francisco Garces, selected the presidio site on the east bank of the Santa Cruz River, giving a little security to the region. Mexico won independence from Spain in 1821, and Arizona and New Mexico remained part of the territory of Mexico. A war between the United States and Mexico ended with the signing of the Treaty of Guadalupe Hidalgo of 1848, but Tucson, south of the Gila River, was still part of its southern neighbor's territory.

In 1853, James Gadsden negotiated the purchase of 29,670 square miles, and Tucson became a possession of the United States, as did the remainder of the southern portions of Arizona and New Mexico. However, a Mexican garrison remained until March 10, 1856. In 1860, Tucson was still a lawless place, and its brave 350 non-Indian inhabitants were faced with the constant threat of violence. Captain John C. Cremony's written comments give us a clear picture of these hair-raising times:

> Men walked the streets and public squares with double-barreled shotguns and hunted each other as sportsmen hunt for game. In the graveyard of Tucson there were forty-seven graves of white men in 1860, ten years after the events above recited, and of that number only two had died natural deaths, all the rest being murdered in brawls and barroom quarrels.

In 1867, the Old Pueblo became the capital of the newly created Arizona Territory; later, the capital was moved to Phoenix. Law and order finally did prevail as Tucson progressed into the twentieth century, and Arizona achieved statehood in 1912. Today's Tucson, home of the University of Arizona (the city's largest single employer), is a vital city, with excellent restaurants, golf courses, the Tucson Museum of Art complex, the Flandrau Planetarium, and many more attractions to interest all of us.

White Dove.
The magnificent baroque San Xavier del Bac church incorporates Spanish, Byzantine, and Moorish design. Declared a Registered National Historical Landmark in 1963, this fine example of mission architecture is a favorite spot for visitors.

A Little Bit of Paradise.
What better way to end a day than in the whirlpool bath or swimming pool? A quick dip in the morning before touring Tucson is invigorating, too! Green Valley's appeal to retirees and all its visitors is easily apparent in a relaxed and restorative lifestyle.

Day Trips in Tucson

Rather than staying in Tucson, we took I-19 south to Green Valley, about twenty-three miles away. We love to hook up at the Green Valley RV Resort with its dreamlike view of the Santa Rita Mountains. The community is quiet and orderly, heavily populated by snowbirds and retirees, an excellent base for tours of Tucson and the surrounding area. The bubbling spa and large swimming pool are a luxurious respite after the city's hustle and bustle.

On day-long tours we found the city of Tucson easy to navigate, nicely interwoven with its natural setting, playing a legitimate role in our backroads itinerary. The only exception—an important one for newcomers to Tucson—are the so-called "suicide lanes," which run east to west downtown. The streets between Stone Avenue and Alvernon have a center lane that becomes "reversible" between 7:00 A.M. and 9:00 A.M., holding traffic traveling east to west. Conversely, between 4:00 P.M. and 6:00 P.M., the same lanes handle outbound traffic traveling west to east! During these hours, *no* left turns are permitted. The possibilities for catastrophe with a motorhome or trailer on these suicide lanes give rise to what we call RV

Rena Copperman

Hot Air Ballooning.
Arizona is a center for the lofting flights of balloon fanatics. The sunny weather and stable climate provide a perfect environment for practitioners of this daring sport.

paranoia. You know the feeling: your mind runs amok with vivid imaginings of disaster, and your hands get moist as you grip the steering wheel ever harder, wishing you had five sets of eyes to watch the road and the four mirrors of your RV. Some RVers have told us it helps to sing, but we enjoy cursing "mutant drivers."

Actually the city isn't all that bad to drive in; we emerged unscathed from our tours in Tucson, a city whose strong cultural heritage gave us a wealth of clues for further explorations of the state. In Tucson's museums, we found an abundance of excellent material on Southwestern cultural and natural history.

Tucson's Museums—Fonts of Knowledge

Two museums in particular are really excellent and can provide a broad foundation of knowledge.

Arizona State Museum   The first is the Arizona State Museum, on the grounds of the University of Arizona. The surrounding campus is impressive and worth a stroll, especially through the old section near the museums.

Star Gazing.
The Flandrau Planetarium, located on the campus of the University of Arizona, is one of the major planetaria in the country. The Star Theater features dramatic shows, and space-age exhibits are found in the science halls. The observatory also houses the largest telescope in Arizona intended solely for public use.

At the museum, we saw well-organized and informative exhibits relating to prehistoric and modern Indians. One unique diorama depicts a Paleolithic landscape, including now-extinct Columbian mammoths, camels, antelopes, and bison. It graphically conveys a time 10,000 years ago when the land was verdant with grasslands and oak trees.

Arizona Historical Society/Tucson Museum After acquiring a background in Paleo-Indian and Native American culture, we took a short walk to the Arizona Historical Society/Tucson Museum, just a few blocks from the state museum. It has been designed to show the panorama of Arizona's history, beginning with the Spanish explorers in 1539 and ending with the present. We especially liked the costume hall, rooms executed in the manner of various historic periods, and a copper-mine exhibit where we listened to portable tape recordings that explained the process of copper mining and the life of the miner. There are also excellent research facilities on the premises, as well as huge photo archives.

We enjoyed learning about the story of Pete Kitchen, one of Arizona's most tenacious pioneers. Pete arrived in Arizona in 1855 and built a ranch near Nogales. The five-room adobe ranchhouse had walls twenty-five inches thick, enough to stop the frequent barrages of Apache arrows and rustlers' bullets.

Times were desperate; although his cowboy *vaqueros* were class-A marksmen, Kitchen lost so many hands he created a cemetery on the property. Pete, his beautiful wife, Rosa, his foreman, Manual Ronquillo, and Rosa's brother, Francisco "Pancho" Verdugo, practiced firing blindfolded, probably in a method similar to that of Japanese Zen archers. Although he lost a stepson to an Apache raid, "Pete's Stronghold" took its toll on the Apaches and was eventually given a wide berth by the raiders. Pete died in Tucson on August 5, 1895, and the *Arizona Daily Citizen* reported:

> The funeral was one of the largest ever seen in the city, . . . and so closes the earthly career of one of the most remarkable men that ever faced the frontier dangers of the far Southwest. . . . Keenly alert to his surroundings, a quick and ready shot, he bore nothing else than a charmed life and died in peace, and full of years, surrounded by the comforts of civilization and friends.

A City for Food Lovers

Our stomachs were growling, our minds having digested much of what the museums were trying to tell us. We headed for lunch at one of our favorite Mexican restaurants, El Torero in south Tucson. At our table in the cool, colorfully tiled interior, we were served crisp homemade tortilla chips accompanied by a spicy red salsa to stimulate the taste buds. Varying degrees of hotness in the dishes can be requested and we "like it hot," usually ordering a side order of green jalapeño chiles to further raise the temperature. With gusto we downed bowls of *menudo*, a delicious spicy Mexican tripe soup, and glasses of frosty beer. For dessert we had *sopaipillas* (fritters, southwestern-style) and honey.

Some of our favorite Sonoran dishes (for which Tucson is famous) include *flautas*, thin, crisp tortilla flutes filled with shredded beef or pork covered with guacamole (mashed avocado, onion, tomato, and herbs), with a dab of sour cream. The *chimichanga* is a real Tucson dish, much larger than the flautas, but made also with shredded beef or chicken wrapped in a large flour tortilla and deep fried. This, too, is usually served with guacamole and sour cream. Especially good is a plate of pork *carnitas*, roasted and shredded pork and spices served with hot flour or corn tortillas with a side of refried beans and rice. We also like green corn *tamales*, a meat dish enveloped by a thick ground-corn outer layer and steamed in a corn husk. *Huevos Rancheros* is a great breakfast dish, consisting of eggs, spicy tomatoes, onions, *chorizo* sausage, and tortillas.

Mexican food differs from Texas through Arizona, and each region has its own indigenous dishes or specialties. Tucson has many wonderful Mexican restaurants, and there are literally hundreds claiming to have authentic Sonoran cuisine; many serve only a facsimile. We stay away from the places that make their enchiladas, chimichangas, flautas, or carnitas with ground hamburger meat and melted soft cheese. To some tourists, this is Mexican food, but we prefer shredded meat in these

The University of Arizona was founded in 1891. Six faculty members taught thirty-six students both high-school prep courses and college-level material. The original land was donated by a saloon keeper and two gamblers. Old Main, the first building on campus, dates to about 1900.

Red-hot Ristra.
The chile ristra is a hanging bundle of dried chiles seen everywhere in the Southwest. For lovers of spicy food, the chile is the cornerstone of an exciting regional cuisine.

Buddy Mays

dishes. At the better restaurants, the shredded pork, beef, and chicken are usually marinated in sauce and cooked with fresh chiles, cilantro (Mexican parsley, also known as coriander), and other spices.

Exploring Life in the Desert

With our luncheon feast and visits to two museums under our belts, we wanted to learn more about life in the desert. Our venture took us on a fourteen-mile drive west from downtown Tucson to the Arizona-Sonora Desert Museum (west on Ajo Way, then northwest on Kinney Road).

Opened in 1952 by William Carr, it's a 110-acre regional museum in the Tucson Mountain County Park, devoted to the flora and fauna of the Sonora Desert (annual rainfall of five to ten inches). Over 200 species of live animals and 400 species of plants are displayed in, as the the *New York Times* described it, " . . . probably the most distinctive zoo in the United States . . . a combination of museum, zoo, botanic garden, and nature trail."

Life in the Desert.
A family favorite is the Arizona-Sonora Desert Museum with its abundant exhibits of animals and plants, aquatic life, walk-in aviary, earth sciences center, underwater viewing area, and desert garden abloom with colors.

Arizona-Sonora Desert Museum

Arizona-Sonora Desert Museum

Sonoran Watering Hole.
White-tailed deer are just one of two hundred varieties of animals that make their home in the Arizona-Sonora Desert Museum. The natural habitats display animals in a way that is both aesthetic and humane.

We walked the paths, read the plaques, stood at the overlooks before panoramic desert views, and observed animals and plants in re-creations of their natural ecosystems: subtropical riverine, desert foothill, grassland, and mountain habitat.

Coming into one shadowy shelter, we found ourselves looking through a large window over the shoulders of reclining male and female cougars, sharing a vista of their little "canyon" and the valley beyond. Surely, in our lifetimes, we'll never get closer to these animals. The moment was the high point of our visit to the Arizona-Sonora Desert Museum.

Saguaro National Monument—West Moving on, we drove west on Ajo Road to Kinney Road, then right to the western Saguaro National Monument. If we'd not been camping at the Green Valley RV Resort, we could have parked the motorhome at the Gilbert Ray Campground located in the Tucson Mountain County Park.

The Red Hills Information Center is the national monument headquarters for the western sector. There we found out about tours, the Cactus Garden and Desert Discovery nature trails, and the six-mile Bajada Loop Drive, a graded road that we drove through hilly terrain past saguaro

Arizona-Sonora Desert Museum, Monica DeHart

Rat Trap.
The kestrel is one of the most common birds of prey in the Arizonan deserts. Easily identified by its rufus (the reddish-brown head and back), it lives on a diet of insects and small rodents.

spires. Since Arizona's state flower is the saguaro cactus blossom and its state bird the cactus wren, this national monument takes on special meaning.

Saguaro National Monument—East Saguaro East—the Rincon Mountain Unit—is about twenty-five miles east of Saguaro West—the Tucson Mountain Unit. Together they incorporate 83,576 acres of the Sonora Desert. In Saguaro East, there is a visitor information center and eight-mile-long Cactus Forest Drive through mature saguaro forest. Both sectors offer trails for short and long hikes, and in the Rincon Mountains there are trails accessible only by horse and foot. We were told that these higher-altitude pathways in the Rincon Mountains lead to woodlands of scrub oak and forests of ponderosa pine and Douglas fir, environs similar to the northern United States and Canada. How incredible it seems that within the radius of Tucson is such natural variety.

Great Flora and Fauna Masterfully adapted to the Sonora Desert's aridity and heat, the saguaro cactus starts life as a seed the size of a grain of sand. It can reach a height of fifty feet in 200 years, the largest cactus in the United States. Pleated like an accordion, the plant stores water during the rainy season, expanding when filled. In a single rainfall, a saguaro's vast network of roots can collect as much as 200 gallons of water, enough to supply its needs for a year. The small spines that protrude from the great, green stalks are a protective device for the reserves of water, so attractive to thirsty animals. The cacti, unfortunately, seem to be badly affected by pollution and disruption of natural cycles by human beings.

Arizona-Sonora Desert Museum, Donald Vascimini

Dove of the Desert.
A dove guards its eggs in the arms of a saguaro cactus. The very spines that provide the plant's defense also house and protect nesting birds.

Springtime visitors to Tucson can enjoy the spectacular display of big, white daisylike saguaro flowers decorating the desert from late April to June. For bird-watchers, the Saguaro National Monument provides a chance to observe winged dwellers in the multistoried apartment complexes, vertical aviaries, formed by the cacti. Using the holes of the saguaros, birds such as the Gila woodpecker, gilded flicker, American kestrel, Lucy's warbler, cactus wren, western kingbird, elf owl, screech owl, and purple martin make their homes. As we drove through the stark landscape of dry, saguaro-studded foothills and mountains, the miracle of the desert was easily apparent. We saw past the heat and dryness into the enduring ways of nature.

On the Stage of the Old West

After our first two stops, we decided to have some unadulterated fun at Old Tucson, also located on Kinney Road. We found upon entering the gate that this well-known movie location transcends the tourist-trap category and is a world unto itself. A friendly showgirl, Nadine Karavidas, led us around and posed for pictures as we wandered the streets of the sprawling "Old West" town, stopping to watch a mock gunfight and a stage show in one of the saloons. It was interesting to see the attraction's dusty streets and atmospheric buildings, so often the settings for Western dramas. In the heat of the afternoon, a tall lemonade was refreshing. Around three o'clock, we headed back to Green Valley and the swimming pool. The next day we'd take in some of Tucson's other sights.

Buddy Mays

Glorious Flowers.
The jewels of the desert are its blossoms. Here are lupine and Arizona gold poppies resplendent in purple and orange.

Buddy Mays

Gunslingers' Lament.
Death by lead poisoning is re-enacted daily in Old Tucson. Realistic shootouts take place in the Western movie and television sets as bad guy meets good on the dusty streets.

Into the Wild Blue Yonder

In the morning, we started off our tour with the Pima Air Museum, reached from I-10 eastbound via the Valencia Road exit or from I-10 westbound via the Wilmot Exit. In the vicinity of the Davis-Monthan Air Force Base, we saw a sea of aircraft. Many are being stored and repaired at the base, but on the south side of the road there are over 130 planes that make up the collection of the Pima Air Museum.

It's a staggering sight: the glinting silver wings, the stilled propellers, the echoes of distant wars and flights long ended. Our fighter pilot friend, Herb Meyer, had actually delivered planes to Davis-Monthan, and some of these may have found their way to the Pima Air Museum.

It doesn't take an aeronautics aficionado to appreciate the past preserved here. Small details, such as the collection of World War II fighter pilots' leather jackets, with slogans like "Blood and Guts" painted on the back, are evocative of times gone by but not forgotten. We saw the Boeing B-29 *Superfortress*, the most important high-altitude heavy bomber of WW II (used in Korea as well); the *Enola Gay* and *Bockscar*, both B-29s, dropped the first atomic bombs on Japan in 1945.

Silver Birds.
Once the plane of presidents, this craft now can be toured at the Pima Air Museum. Over eighty years of aviation history are represented here, from a full-scale model of the Wright brothers' 1903 *Wright Flyer* to a mock-up of one of the world's fastest aircraft, the *X-15*.

Of more recent vintage is the presidential aircraft (a DC-6) used by Lyndon Johnson and John Kennedy. It's the only plane here whose interior can be toured. Built in the era immediately preceding the widespread use of computers, the bulkiness of the navigational equipment made us realize just how recently we have entered the age of the microchip. We strolled through some of the 320 acres filled with "aluminum birds," planes whose prototypes were named *Invader, Liberator, Stratojet, Destroyer,* or *Electra.* To a great extent, recreational vehicle construction evolved from light, sturdy, and aerodynamic aluminum airplanes. Our motorhome seemed more than ever a cross between the Conestoga wagon and the *Superfortress.*

Sabino Canyon

With visions of airplanes still before us, we continued our day by going to Sabino Canyon, which can be reached from I-10 via exit 271 and Kolb Road, with a right at Tanque Verde and a left on Sabino Canyon Road. This is a lovely, scenic place in the Santa Catalina foothills, once the stomping ground of Colombian mammoths some 12,000 years ago. Hohokam Indians built irrigation dams on the creek in A.D. 1200. Later, in the 1870s,

Magical Canyon.
In Tucson's Santa Catalina Mountains, Sabino Canyon is a magnificent spot to explore.

Robert J. Smith

Idyllic Hiking.
Sabino Canyon's streams and waterfalls provide a lush reminder of more aqueous climates. Hikers can ride from the parking area to lower Bear Canyon by bus, then hike 4.4 miles round-trip to Seven Falls.

cavalry soldiers from Fort Lowell rode in to swim on hot summer days, and in the 1930s, workers from the Civilian Conservation Corps built bridges and 3.8 miles of road into the Santa Catalina Mountains. Pressures of the modern world have made necessary the present-day environmental protection of the canyon, but we talked of Jim's Arizona boyhood and memorable teenage years when he lived on Sabino Canyon Road and rode his horse up into the wilderness without restriction, stopping by Seven Falls. Today's visitors park their vehicles and hike or take shuttle buses with a narrated tour. These buses run 365 days a year.

Arizona Office of Tourism

Mt. Lemmon.
A refreshing change lies in the heights of Tucson's favorite getaway mountain. The 7,000-foot rise in altitude produces changes in flora, like those between southern Arizona and the Canadian border. In winter, with sufficient snow, Mt. Lemmon is the most southerly skiing facility in the nation.

Mount Lemmon

Mount Lemmon is also in the Santa Catalinas, and you can get there by going east on Tanque Verde until it connects with Hitchcock Highway. The thirty-mile pull up to Mount Lemmon's 9,157-foot summit is an hour-long trip. We did not have time to make the climb and can only suggest that it might be wise to use a car for the day trip if one doesn't have a small recreational vehicle. Larger RVs and trailers can be difficult to navigate on winding mountainous roads. In our wanderings, there have been tight spots from time to time, as in the cramped campground at the Chiricahua National Monument or the White Mountains' infamous Zane Grey's cabin (where no turnaround room is provided for large RVs at the end of a remote dirt road).

Colossal Cave

For spelunkers, Colossal Cave, to the southeast of Tucson on the Old Spanish Trail Road past the Saguaro National Monument, offers intricate displays of crystal formations. Billed as "Arizona's Greatest Underground Natural Wonder," the attraction is twenty-two miles from downtown Tucson. Also known as the largest dry cave in the world, Colossal Cave stretches into the Rincon Mountains, its extent still unknown. With a constant temperature of 72°F, it's almost twenty degrees warmer than Carlsbad Caverns in New Mexico, and far smaller (an admission fee is charged).

White Dove of the Desert

Swinging around back to I-19, and en route to Green Valley, we stopped at Mission San Xavier del Bac, the "the White Dove of the Desert," in the Santa Cruz Valley, nine miles south of Tucson. It's one of those visionary sights that's hauntingly beautiful, a beacon in the desert.

In the 1700s, it was a jewel in the strand of missions established by the Spaniards in the early colonial days. San Xavier evokes the area's Spanish colonial past with a grace rivaled perhaps only by the church at Tumacacori (see page 50). It's truly an architectural poem in its rugged desert setting and is considered the paramount example of mission architecture in the United States.

We drove to it from I-19 through the Tohono O'Odham (Papago) Indians' San Xavier Indian Reservation, their home for centuries. *Bac,* the word for "the place where water appears," refers to the Santa Cruz River, which is partly subterranean but surfaces near the site of the mission.

The Great Father Kino Father Eusebio Francisco Kino was initially responsible for San Xavier's creation. A renowned Jesuit missionary and explorer, he came to Bac in 1692 and later again in 1700. His efforts produced the foundation of the first church, located two miles north of the mission's present site. It was called San Xavier after Father Kino's patron saint, St. Francis Xavier, the famed Jesuit "Apostle of the Indies."

The style of the present San Xavier Mission is a combination of Moorish, Byzantine, and late-Mexican Renaissance influences that combine harmoniously in a structure of domes and arches with wooden window and door frames. The interior testifies to the mystical power of Catholicism. We really enjoyed the original artwork and reliquaries in the church's interior; there seemed to be murals and paintings everywhere we looked, as well as aged statues of saints and flickering votive candles. It was a wonderful immersion in the visual pageantry sustaining the spiritual lives of the Southwest's first Spaniards.

Such pageantry can be witnessed on the first Friday after Easter during the annual San Xavier Festival. The celebration honors the mission's founding with a gathering of costumed "Spanish horsemen," berobed priests, mesquite bonfires, Tohono O'Odham dances, and a variety of crafts and food booths.

Queen of Mission Architecture.
Mission San Xavier del Bac can be seen
from far away, one of its two towers still
uncompleted. Whether this was done to
avoid a Spanish tax on completed churches
or as a memorial to a dead architect, no
one knows. The rich decoration of statuary
and painting inside is belied by the simple
lines of the mission's exterior.

European Influence.
The architecture of the exterior facade of Mission San Xavier del Bac reminds one of a European church. The intricate carving and statue of a king seem almost out of place in the desert. Yet, San Xavier symbolizes the coming together of Spain, the Catholic Church, and Native Americans.

Robert J. Smith

Backroad to Green Valley

We took the Mission Road back down to Green Valley, driving straight ahead as we left San Xavier to the Duval Mine Road. At Duval, we turned left and soon came to the entrance of the Green Valley RV Resort. Our exploration of Tucson had readied us for further travels in southern Arizona.

POINTS OF INTEREST: Arizona Tour 2

The Tucson Area

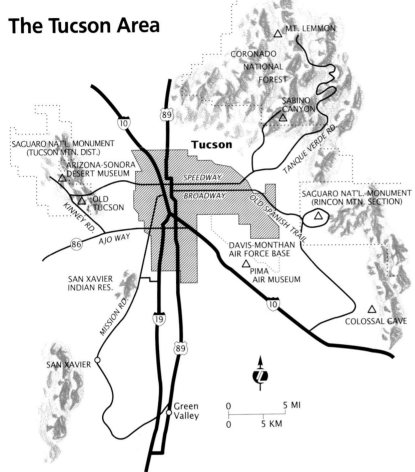

Buddy Mays

ACCESS: North *I-10* and *US 89*; south, *I-19* and *US 89*; east, *I-10*; west, *SR 86*.

INFORMATION: *Tucson Metropolitan Chamber of Commerce*, 465 W. St. Mary's Road, P.O. Box 991, Tucson 85701 (602) 792-2250; *Green Valley Chamber of Commerce*, 101-73 S. La Canada, P.O. Box 566, Green Valley 85614 (602) 625-7575.

ANNUAL EVENTS:

Tucson: *Tucson International Gem and Mineral Extravaganza*, Tucson Convention Center; *Tucson Balloon Festival*; *La Fiesta de Los Vaqueros* (biggest midwinter rodeo in America), February; *Fourth Avenue Street Fair* (3-day crafts show), April and December; *Cinco de Mayo*, Kennedy Park; *Tucson Arts Festival*, May.

SPECIAL ATTRACTIONS:

Sabino Canyon Tours, Inc., Route 15, Box 280, Tucson 85715 (602) 749-2861, information and tour schedules; (602) 749-2327 (moonlight tour reservations and group rates).

RESTAURANTS:

Tucson has hundreds of restaurants. Get the free booklet, *Dining in the Desert*, from the Southern Arizona Restaurant Association, Chamber of Commerce Building, 465 W. St. Mary's Rd., Suite 300, Tucson 85701, (602) 791-9106.

NEARBY ATTRACTIONS:

San Xavier del Bac, I-19 to Valencia Rd., west to Mission Rd. (602) 294-2624. Masses: Mon.–Sat. 8:30 A.M.; Sunday 8:00 A.M., 11:00 A.M., 12:30 P.M.

MUSEUMS & GALLERIES:

Tucson: *Arizona State Museum*, University of Arizona campus (602) 621-6302, Monday–Saturday 9 A.M.–5 P.M., Sunday 2 P.M.–5 P.M., free; *Arizona Historical Society*, Tucson Museum, 949 E. Second St. 85719 (602) 628-5774, Monday–Saturday 10 A.M.–4 P.M., Sunday noon–4 P.M., free; *Arizona-Sonora Desert Museum*, 2021 N. Kinney Rd. (602) 883-1380, daily 8:30 A.M.–6 P.M., admission charge; *Pima Air Museum*, 6000 E. Valencia Rd. 85706 (602) 574-9658, daily 9 A.M.–5 P.M., last admission 4 P.M., admission charge; *Tucson Museum of Art*, 140 N. Main Ave. 85701 (602) 624-2333, Tuesday–Saturday 10 A.M.–4 P.M., Sunday 1–4 P.M., free Tuesday, (crafts, textiles, furniture, fine arts); *Center for Creative Photography*, University of Arizona campus (602) 621-7968, Monday–Friday 10 A.M.–5 P.M., summer, noon to 5 P.M., free (photo exhibits, large photo library); *Grace H. Flandrau Planetarium*, University of Arizona campus, Cherry Ave., (602) 621-4515, show information 621-STAR, Monday–Friday 10 A.M.– P.M., Saturday–Sunday 1 P.M.–5 P.M., Tuesday–Saturday 7 P.M.–9 P.M., admission charge for theater only.

MEXICO'S BORDERLANDS
The Spanish Colonial Loop

The rich Tombstone mines brought bad men from all parts of the West into the valleys of the San Simon, Sulphur Spring, and San Pedro Rivers, where stage robbers, outlaws, and cattle thieves found refuge. But for all that, Tombstone was an orderly, law-abiding town. What little killing was done there was done among the lawless element themselves.

William M. Breakenridge,
Helldorado

Buddy Mays

From the Green Valley base, we planned to day-trip in southeastern Arizona through an especially flamboyant past: Eras of exploration by Alvar Nunez Cabeza de Vaca and Francisco Vasquez de Coronado; the period of Spanish colonialism; and copper- and gold-mining days in the nineteenth century.

Into the Santa Ritas

The desert was still cool on the morning we set out with unofficial tour guide, John D. Vincent, mining engineer, long-time Arizona resident, and Jim's dad. His wife, Margaret, is mountain man Joe Walker's great-great niece (Walker was a legendary figure throughout the West and led an expedition of prospectors to Prescott, Arizona). We were in good hands on the backroad (known as the Greaterville Road) from Green Valley; it starts at Continental and heads into the Santa Rita Mountains and the Coronado National Forest, bypassing the turn for Madera Canyon. Climbing and winding past deep, narrow canyons, we saw a group of bird-watchers gathered by a small stream, eyes straining through binoculars as they searched enthusiastically for feathered friends. Incidentally, an excellent map of hiking trails around Madera Canyon is published by the Friends of Madera Canyon, a group affiliated with the Green Valley Hiking Club.

After bumping over this one-lane canyon backroad, we voted the route advisable only for recreational vehicles under fourteen feet, trucks, or cars. Several stretches might imperil a larger motorhome or trailer; the canyons of the Santa Ritas are quite remote and rugged.

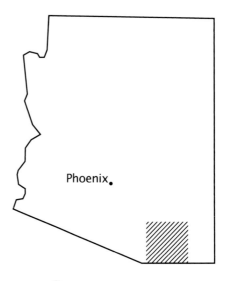

Phoenix.

Tour **3** *215 miles*

SANTA RITA MOUNTAINS • GREATERVILLE • SONOITA • TOMBSTONE • BISBEE • CORONADO NATIONAL MEMORIAL • SIERRA VISTA • FORT HUACHUCA • PATAGONIA • NOGALES • TUMACACORI • TUBAC

High Plains Gold Country

Greaterville and Sonoita

The dusty backroad eventually became a paved one and then ended at SR 83 where we turned south, driving toward Greaterville and Sonoita beyond it. Greaterville was the locale of the Santa Ritas' first gold strike in 1874; the town, with a population of 500 in the 1870s, was a center, not only for miners, but also for cowboys, some of them *vaqueros* from the huge Empire Ranch. The jail was literally a hole in the ground, miscreants lowered into it by rope. Greaterville was located on a road known as Renegades Route, a path from the Mexican border used by fugitives from the law.

At Sonoita, a miniscule junction, we turned eastward on SR 82 across the high desert plain to Tombstone. After our ascent up the Santa Ritas' cramped canyons, we found ourselves on a windswept plateau with the crowning points of mountains ringing the golden high-desert plains.

Panning for Gold.
A solitary miner pans for gold near Tombstone, where once more than 600 people lived in a tent mining-city clustered around one very unglamorous saloon.

Mountain Battlement.
The Santa Rita Mountains in the Coronado National Forest lie between the Empire Mountains to the north and the Patagonia Mountains to the south. We reached the high-desert plain of Tombstone by climbing the unforgiving backroad known as the Greaterville Road. An alternate route to Tombstone is via I-10 east to SR 83 south to Sonoita.

When Tombstone was the West's wildest mining town, 110 saloons operated around the clock. Today there are five saloons left, including the Crystal Palace, which still mixes its own sarsaparilla and has raised the price of a shot of whiskey from 12¢ to $2 in the past 100 years.

The Town Too Tough to Die

The wind seemed to sweep us across the grasslands as we approached Tombstone, the legendary town that, more than any other, symbolizes the Wild West. Having turned down US 80, we rolled into the outskirts, where the famed cemetery, Boothill, awaits on the left side of the road. We toured the famous burial ground, the final resting place for 180 souls. Tombstone's heyday lasted for approximately eight years in the 1870s and 1880s, and the gravestones illustrate the past. Walking through the stark white memorials, we read the sometimes bizarre epitaphs of those who had died there, feeling the humor, desperation, and poignancy in the inscriptions:

"Here Lies Lester More, Four Slugs from a 44, No Les, No More."

"John Heath, Taken from County Jail 8, Lynched by a Bisbee Mob, Feb 22 1884."

"Al Bennett, Ambushed by Apaches."

"Marshall White, Shot by Curly Bill."

The simple obituaries describe a society fraught with frequent hangings, Indian attacks, and shootouts, and possessing a population of Chi-

The Endless Road.
State Road 82 leads from Sonoita to US 80 and Tombstone, traversing the windswept spaces of elevated grasslands surrounded by mountain peaks.

nese workers. A walk on Boothill is certainly a detour through life as it was in the old West.

The Tombstone Courthouse   After soaking up the graveyard's atmosphere of mortality, we drove into town. True, Tombstone proper has its commercial side, but very interesting and entirely genuine is the Tombstone Courthouse, now a State Historic Park. Situated on a one-acre plot, the park is the smallest in the state. While walking through displays of environs and memorabilia from the late nineteenth century, we found it easy to absorb a sense of times past from the court room, post office, various firearms, a faro table and the implements of the game, and Indian and ranching artifacts.

This grand old courthouse was built in 1882 and was the first permanent seat of government for Cochise County; it's a huge Victorian building with high ceilings. We walked through the halls, almost hearing the sounds of a gavel rapping or a trapdoor falling. Outside in the old jail's exercise yard sits a reconstruction of the original gallows that we couldn't resist walking underneath.

On the first floor, there is also a case with a picture of Ed Schieffelin, the prospector whose silver lodes, the Lucky Cuss, Grand Central, and

Contention, were the beginning of Tombstone. He was known from coast to coast as the man who made the biggest silver strike in Arizona history. Even today there are tours in Tombstone through an original Schieffelin mine, the Goodenough.

The OK Corral and the Bird Cage Theatre Driving around town, we found the commercialism irksome but understandable, given the economics of the area. If you disregard the mild exploitation of local history, you'll enjoy the OK Corral, at one time a vacant lot, where the Earps and the Clantons had their infamous gunfight. A marvelous landmark is the Bird Cage Theatre, a saloon and dance hall built in 1881 and unrivaled as the "the wildest, wickedest nightspot between Basin Street and the Barbary Coast" (*New York Times*, 1882) until 1889. Suspended from the ceiling, fourteen velvet-draped "bird cage" crib compartments sheltered prostitutes plying their trade. Down below, there was the cacophonous din of drinking, gambling, music, can-can dancers, and occasional violence. In the basement's poker room, one game lasted eight years, five months, and three days, the longest in Western history.

After its glory days, the Bird Cage was closed for fifty years, preserving the original fixtures, furniture, and interior for the future. It's now a registered National Monument at 6th and Allen streets. The world's largest rose tree can also be found here, in the patio of the Rose Tree Inn.

Architectural Bonanza.
The Cochise County Courthouse is a masterpiece of Art Deco design. Dedicated in 1931 and finished with copious amounts of mahogany, marble, and copper, it houses a large relief map of Cochise County.

Where Copper Reigned Supreme

From Tombstone, we continued driving south on US 80 to Bisbee, passing through the one-third-mile-long Mule Pass Tunnel and the Mule Mountains, eager to stop for lunch at The Copper Queen Hotel.

In the 1880s, Bisbee was a boomtown that developed around the Copper Queen Mine; it seemed little changed when we stopped on the hill above, looking down at the fabled hamlet, some of it crammed into two ravines (Tombstone Canyon or Main Street and Brewery Gulch) and propped precariously on surrounding hillsides. Nestled below us was the downtown section, now included on the National Register of Historic Places. Just a little farther south on SR 80 is the enormous Lavender Pit Mine, but back up in Bisbee the variety of architecture boggles the mind. For anyone interested in a hundred years of art and design, there is a little bit of everything, from turn-of-the-century grandeur to Art Deco. There is also the Bisbee Mining and Historical Museum in the old Phelps-Dodge offices at 5 Copper Queen Plaza. With our backgrounds in art, we took special pleasure in the nuances of design, such as the copper-colored face above the front door of the beautifully restored Copper Queen Hotel.

Our tour guide, not only an authority on copper extraction but a gourmet cook, led us to one of the great eateries of Cochise County, the Copper Queen Hotel, appearing much as it did when opened in 1902. The Copper Queen is an old hotel and excellent eatery and like Bisbee has an atmosphere rich as a mother lode of copper. We ate as Jim's father entertained us with tales of the early days of mining in southeastern Arizona.

Famed Eatery.
Built in 1902, the Copper Queen Hotel was a truly opulent hotel in its heyday. Many luminaries graced its premises, including President Teddy Roosevelt and General John "Blackjack" Pershing. The restaurant still serves excellent fare; the hotel has barely changed.

Mining Lore and Art

For RVers who wish to delve more deeply into mining lore, Bisbee has underground and open-pit mine tours, as well as minibus excursions around the town. The latter are advisable since parking is scarce and the streets of Bisbee narrow. We noticed an RV park on the south side of US 80, but those facilities looked confining as well. Despite such logistical difficulties, Bisbee is a fascinating potpourri from a time when mining

Unrivaled Copper Camp.
Bisbee was a mother lode of wealth over its ninety-five years of continuous operation. Statistics note the production of 8,032,352,000 pounds of copper, 2,871,786 ounces of gold, 77,162,986 ounces of silver, 304,627,600 pounds of lead, and 371,945,900 pounds of zinc!

wealth created a cosmopolitan boomtown in the heart of Apache Indian country. We could sense its unique isolation and rarefied cultural atmosphere. For the aesthetically inclined, a longer stay might be pleasantly invested in poking about the streets and buildings here. But in our one-day-loop tour, time was limited.

Coronado National Memorial

At the junction of Bisbee, we had the option to go southwest seventeen miles on SR 92, turning off at Montezuma Canyon Road. It's then six miles to the Coronado National Memorial, situated in the vicinity of the first European expedition on southwestern soil. Hiking, bird-watching, and a view of Mexico reward the wanderer to this remote national monument. The memorial was built to honor Francisco Vasquez de Coronado's 1540 entrance into what are now U.S. lands, but Coronado was not the first European.

Alvar Núñez Cabeza de Vaca

One of the most interesting stories of the first European forays into southern Arizona is that found in *Los Naufragios* (1542), the account by Alvar

Núñez Cabeza de Vaca. This journal of the years 1527–1537 tells of an expedition to Florida under an inept and cruel leader, Pánfilo de Narváez. Cabeza de Vaca was second in command of the ill-fated odyssey. After landing near present-day Tampa, Florida, Narváez made the classic military error of splitting his cavalry and troops from their supply ships and set off up the coast of Florida. The expedition continued from central Florida in log barges, across the Gulf of Mexico, where several men lost their lives and the survivors were captured and enslaved by various Indian groups along the Texas gulf coast.

After several years, out of the original 300 men only Cabeza de Vaca, Alonzo del Castillo Maldonado, Andrés Dorantes, and Dorante's Moorish slave, Esteban, survived to meet the Pima Indians in the vicinity of what is known as Bisbee. Toward the end of their journey in what is present-day western New Mexico and Arizona, the four became faith healers to the various groups of Indians. The Indians treated them as messengers of the gods, bringing their sick and wounded to them, and in many cases experiencing miraculous cures. This was at a time when Christians had barbaric ways of treating native inhabitants.

While Cabeza de Vaca returned to Spain, Esteban the Moor backtracked to Arizona with a Franciscan priest, Fray Marcos de Niza. Esteban separated from him and was killed by members of a Zuni pueblo, near what is today the northern Arizona–New Mexico border. (Indian guides who survived the melee said Esteban was killed because he boasted pompously of his divine nature and insulted the Zuni by demanding the tribal women.)

Wild Peccary.
The hardy javelina *(Tayassu tajacu)* is a well-known citizen of Arizona's arid lands. These small piglike animals weigh about fifty pounds and eat roots, fruit, insects, worms, and reptiles.

Seven Cities of Gold

The good Fray Marcos returned to Mexico with fantastic tales that added fuel to the wishful Spanish myth of Seven Cities of Gold (Cibola) and a northwest passage to the Orient, not to mention the thousands of barbarian souls to be saved or at least enslaved.

Subsequently an expedition led by Francisco Vasquez de Coronado was launched in February, 1540, but after failing to find the golden cities, Coronado returned to Mexico in disgrace. Although he didn't find the gold, history has vindicated Coronado and hailed him as one of the world's great explorers.

Sierra Vista and Fort Huachuca

We left Bisbee after lunch, driving north on US 80 and veering west on SR 90 toward Sierra Vista, a modern town with shopping malls and recreational vehicle parks—an excellent place for RVers to restock the larder.

Sierra Vista is the bedroom community for the massive army base at Fort Huachuca (we passed it on SR 90), founded at the foot of the Huachuca (or Thunder) Mountains in 1877 during the Indian wars. The base allows visitors to picnic and hike in Garden Canyon and the Huachuca Mountains.

Buddy Mays

Winged Whirlwind.
The tiny hummingbird is prevalent in the Mile Hi/Ramsey Canyon Preserve. The hummingbird flies at speeds up to sixty miles an hour with wingbeats from fifty to seventy-five beats a second. At night, having expended so much energy, they fall into a torpor similar to hibernation.

Hummingbird Heaven

The Mile Hi/Ramsey Canyon Preserve, the Nature Conservancy's 300-acre wooded park, lies in a sheltered gorge in the Huachucas, just five miles southeast of Sierra Vista. This is a favorite spot of bird-watchers, where fourteen species of hummingbirds (a number exceeded nowhere else in the United States) have been observed and recorded in photographs. The preserve is open from 8:00 A.M. to 5:00 P.M., but reservations are required for weekends and holidays due to limited parking space. Call (602) 378-2785 for reservations.

We drove up SR 90, turning southwest on SR 82, past Sonoita into Patagonia, a little town in a charmingly beautiful area; the road runs through a canyon and wooded areas with green trees watered by a small stream. The beautiful harlequin or Mearns quail, proudly dressed in black-and-white feathers and a polka-dotted breast, inhabits this area of Arizona.

Patagonia

Our arrival in tiny Patagonia brought us to a hotel bar, a cool drink, and a moment's relaxation. Soon we ventured forth on the main street to locate Patagonia's Stradling Museum of the Horse, one of the stranger conglomerations of artifacts we saw in our travels. Collected by Ann Stradling, the museum's six large rooms are filled to overflowing with items from all over the world; the estimated value is $4 million. Included in the collection are a Conestoga wagon, a Roman chariot, a Mexican ox cart, as well as innumerable horse-related items. In other rooms, there are many Indian objects, including a fascinating kachina doll collection. The museum has its share of paintings, too. We saw works by Frederic Remington and Charles Russell, as well as fancy, carved Mexican saddles and bridles of every description.

Nogales

Southward on SR 82, we passed through the outskirts of Nogales and then cut back up north on I-19. Nogales is not the sleepy little Mexican border town we had imagined. It's an important economic center, especially for manufacturing contacts between Mexico and the United States, and as a shipping point for imported fruits and vegetables. The border towns are called *Ambos Nogales*, the Mexican side having a far larger population. Both are located in a mountain pass, a conduit for commerce since prehistoric times. North Americans can sample life south of the border without needing a passport or tourist card and (after 48 hours) return with $400 worth of goods, duty-free, and one liter of liquor. Both sides of the border have some excellent Mexican restaurants. Casa Molina, located on the old Pete Kitchen ranch near I-19, serves homemade *carne seca*, a dish made from dried or jerked beef, cooked again in a spicy sauce. It's one of our favorites, and we both ordered it.

Festive Borderland.
Nogales, situated in Arizona, and her Mexican counterpart, *Ambos Nogales,* are bustling towns that offer shopping adventures on both sides of the border.

Robert Longsdorf

Peña Blanca Lake

Eight miles north of Nogales and seven miles west on SR 289 lies Peña Blanca Lake, nestled in a mountainous section of the Coronado National Forest. The lake has good fishing for largemouth bass, bluegill, crappie, catfish, and trout and offers a welcome respite from the desert. For RVers of like mind, Peña Blanca Lake might provide a good restorative; at the state-run recreational area, there's RV camping and a German restaurant.

At the Crossroads.
Tumacacori National Monument is a frontier mission-church near Tubac where five cultures and seven flags have played out numerous dramas over hundreds of years. The monument relates the saga of early Indian and Spanish history, as well as describing the style of life around Tumacacori and the surrounding territory.

Tumacacori

We continued on north ten miles from the turn-off to Peña Blanca on I-19 to Tumacacori National Monument (San Jose de Tumacacori), built by mission priests in the 1700s. We went through the visitor center and museum, and out through a door to the mission building, a magnificent relic of European influence and native ingenuity.

Tumacacori was one of the ships in the armada of missions built to defend Christian faith in the New World and to perpetuate Spain's influence in the province of Sonora. Sites for early religious outposts were established by the Jesuits, and the remains of Tumacacori and stalwart mission buildings elsewhere bear witness to remarkable courage and conviction by their architects and builders. The first symbolic brick was laid in 1691, when Father Eusebio Kino arrived in what is now southern Arizona. He was an Italian Jesuit, educated in Germany, who spent from 1687 to his death in 1711 exploring and mapping the upper Pima country. In 1794, a Spanish Franciscan, Father Narciso Gutierrez, came to the small Pima village of Tumacacori and resurrected the church, hoping to build one that might rival the magnificence of San Xavier del Bac. The history of the mission reflects the many transitions that have taken place in southern Arizona. Exhibits in the park museum shed light on life in the days of early Indian and Spanish history and the park is open from 8:00 A.M. to 5:00 P.M.

One of our favorite Mexican restaurants, Wisdom's, is located here. They specialize in huge shredded beef or chicken *chimichangas* and also make a delicious fruit *burro* (much like a turnover).

Tubac

Driving a few miles north up I-19, we came to the sleepy little town of Tubac set against the gorgeous backdrop of the Santa Rita Mountains. Periodically, Tubac's longevity has been precarious. Now its charm and setting have insured survival. It's a thriving artists' colony with numerous galleries and a few restaurants. We saw marvelous pottery and folk art from around the world in one store. The town is part of the area's Hispanic past.

The Presidio

After Father Kino's establishment of Tumacacori, Tubac, originally a Pima village, became a *visita* or mission farm where Spaniards settled. During a Pima revolt in 1751, the Spanish were pushed southward, but after peace

A Creative Center.
Tubac has a wealth of shops—over fifty dedicated to fine arts, crafts, and unusual gifts. The work of both local artisans and crafts from foreign countries delight visiting shoppers.

A Stellar View.
The Smithsonian's Whipple Observatory
sits at 8,200 feet in the Santa Rita Mountains. Green Valley's clear, dry air enhances
the possibilities for astronomical
observation.

was reestablished by soldiers, a fort, the Presidio de San Ignacio de Tubac,
was founded in June, 1752. Over the years, Tubac was inhabited and
periodically abandoned due to Apache attacks or economic conditions;
this ebb and flow discouraged stable growth or settlement.

We strolled around the archaeological excavation of the Presidio begun
in 1874 by the University of Arizona. The Tubac Presidio State Historic
Park encompasses the old presidio site and an underground interpretive
display; the museum contains Spanish artifacts and implements of daily
life. There's also an 1885 schoolhouse.

Homeward Bound

It had been a long and lovely day. After our circuitous travels in southeastern Arizona, we watched the soft evening light define myriad bright
colors on the rocky faces of the mountains and basked in the beauty as we
drove north on I-19, enjoying a splendid view of Mount Wrightson and the
observatory on Mount Hopkins in the Santa Ritas (run by the Smithsonian
Institution, which also offers bus tours to the mountaintop and the
observatory).

POINTS OF INTEREST: Arizona Tour 3

The Spanish Colonial Loop

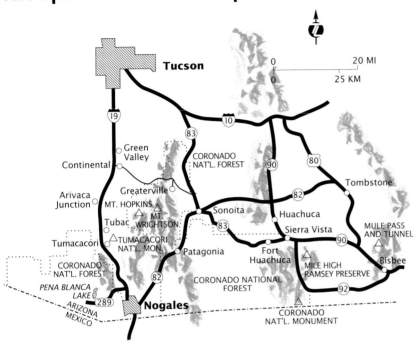

ACCESS: From Green Valley via Continental, backroad (known as the *Greaterville Road*) through the Santa Ritas bypassing Madera Canyon.

INFORMATION: *Green Valley Chamber of Commerce*, Continental Shopping Plaza, P.O. Box 566, Green Valley 85622 (602) 625-7575; *Tombstone Tourism Association*, P.O. Box 917, Tombstone 85638 (602) 457-2211; *Greater Bisbee Chamber of Commerce*, 7 Naco Rd., P.O. Drawer BA, Bisbee 85603 (602) 432-2141; *Sierra Vista Area Chamber of Commerce*, 77 Calle Portal, No. 140A, Sierra Vista 85635 (602) 458-6940; *Nogales-Santa Cruz County Chamber of Commerce*, Kino Park, Nogales 85621 (602) 287-3685.

ANNUAL EVENTS:

Bisbee: *La Vuelta de Bisbee* (3-day bicycle race), April; *Bisbee Art Festival* (local arts and crafts), September; *Bisbee Fine Art Miniature Show*, December.

Tombstone: *Tombstone Territorial Days* (a birthday celebration, pet parade, firehouse cart races), March; *Rendezvous of Gunfighters* (shows at OK Corral, parade of 1880s characters), September.

Tubac: *Festival of the Arts*, February.

Tumacacori: *Annual Festival* (folk dancing, music of the Santa Cruz Valley's cultural groups), December.

MUSEUMS & GALLERIES:

Bisbee: *Bisbee Mining and Historical Museum*, 5 Copper Queen Plaza, Monday–Saturday 10 A.M.–4 P.M., Sunday 1 P.M.–4 P.M., (602) 432-7071.

Patagonia: *The Museum of the Horse*, daily (except national holidays) 9 A.M.–5 P.M.

Tombstone: *Tombstone Courthouse*, State Historic Park, 219 Toughnut St., Tombstone 85638 (602) 457-3311.

Tubac: *Tubac Center of the Arts*, (602) 398-2371 Tuesday–Saturday 10 A.M.–4:30 P.M., Sunday 1:00–4:30 P.M.; *Tubac Presidio State Historic Park*, daily 8 A.M.–5 P.M. (except Christmas); (602) 398-2252

Tumacacori: *Tumacacori National Monument* (every weekend native Indian and Mexican craftspeople give demonstrations of native arts) daily 8 A.M.–5 P.M.

SPECIAL ATTRACTIONS:

Tombstone: *Boothill Graveyard* (burial ground of the notorious gold-mining town); *Bird Cage Theatre*, 6th and Allen streets (a registered National Monument), daily.

RESTAURANTS:

Bisbee: *Cow Palace*, Exit 48, Arivaca Junction, (602) 398-2201; *Copper Queen Hotel*, 11 Howell Ave., around the corner from Brewery Gulch, (602) 432-2216.

Patagonia: *The Ovens of Patagonia*, Naugle Ave./Hwy 82, (602) 394-2078, bakery, fresh breads, sweets, sandwiches, pizza on Fridays, open Thursday–Sunday.

VALLEY OF THE SUN
The Phoenix Circle

*This grand old relic . . . looms up over the desert
in bold relief as the traveller approaches, filling
the mind with a strange perplexity as to the past.
What race dwelt here? by what people were these
crumbling walls put together? how did they live?
and where are they gone? were questions that
we were reluctant to believe must forever remain
unanswered; and yet modern research has not
to this day approached a solution to the mystery.*

J. Ross Browne,
Adventures in the Apache Country

Buddy Mays

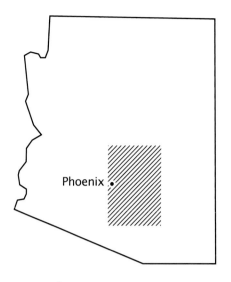

Phoenix, the major metropolitan area of Arizona, may not fit the backroad image, but we mustered our courage and went there because there's so much to see and do in the capital city. We found ways to soften our visit (staying in Mesa and traveling on freeways), but our impressions of rampaging vehicles and traffic jams were still intense.

Pinal Pioneer Highway

We drove to Phoenix from Tucson via the Pinal Pioneer Parkway (US 89). The drive was a peaceful, refreshing trip on a two-lane highway through the Sonora Desert. The cacti were blooming, and little signs identifying the plant life—catclaw, prickly pear, and yucca—had been posted strategically along the road.

Catalina State Park

Just outside Tucson, we stopped at Catalina State Park, which has fifty sites and is open year-round. There is water available and a dump station, but no hookups. The Santa Catalina Mountains rise up and provide a gorgeous setting in which to camp. This would be a first-rate place to stay while touring the Tucson area.

Tom Mix Monument

Further on, we passed the Tom Mix Monument, which memorializes silent film's Tom Mix and his horse, Tony. Famed during the 1920s for his amazing stunts and horsemanship, many of Mix's films were shot in Arizona. Tom Mix died in 1940, crashing his Cord automobile near Florence. The monument came as a colorful, yet poignant, surprise in the midst of so much picturesque desert country.

Casa Grande Ruins National Monument

Proceeding via US 89 to SR 287 (watch for signs saying Casa Grande National Monument), we turned west and drove to the turnoff for Coolidge. North of Coolidge, off SR 87, lies Casa Grande Ruins National Monument. We had long wanted to see one of the Southwest's greatest architectural enigmas, a focal point for archaeological studies of the agrarian Hohokam, creators of an extensive irrigation canal system before the time of Christ. Hohokam is a Pima Indian word meaning, variously, "those who have gone," "all used up," or "vanished ones." Today's Tohono O'Odham (Papago) and Pima Indians (Ackimoel, pronounced Ah-kee-mult, O'Odham, meaning "the river people") are probably their descendants.

Tour **4** *280 miles*

PINAL PIONEER PARKWAY • CASA GRANDE RUINS NATIONAL MONUMENT • PHOENIX • THE APACHE TRAIL

Summer Sunset.
Summers provide the most magnificent desert sunsets. After a sudden rain, visitors can enjoy the brilliant colors of the sinking sun as it outlines a spectacular saguaro cactus on the Apache Trail.

The ancestors of the Hohokam may have come from Mexico to the Gila and Santa Cruz river valleys by 1300 B.C., traveling to the Salt River Valley by 700 B.C. Perhaps each of us must come to a personal conclusion, but anyone who's seen the Mexican ruin of Casas Grandes, 300 kilometers south of El Paso, Texas, or Mayan ruins, such as those at Chichén Itzá or Uxmal, will find similarities between the Hohokam and other Western Hemisphere Indian groups. Curiously, in the Southwest and Mexico we've found a common legend within various Indian mythologies concerning a bearded god-man with fair skin: Quetzalcoatl of the Aztecs and I'Itoi of the Papago (both were killed by their own people). Maybe the forebears of the Hohokam migrated north, maybe not. To amateur archaeologists like us, the comings and goings of these long-gone people are tantalizing; the mystery of the past is a great part of its fascination. The more ruins we visited, the more intrigued we became.

In any case, the Hohokam culture reached its height in A.D. 1200, but by 1450 the Indians had vacated the Salt River Valley. Some scientists, analyzing this exodus, think that soils exhausted by extensive irrigation became too alkaline for growing the cotton and barley that the Hohokam introduced here. Others believe nomadic raiding Indians and social upheaval

Eternal Mystery.
The 650-year-old edifice known as Casa Grande perplexes archaeologists today almost as much as it did European explorers in the seventeenth century. The monument grounds have about sixty prehistoric sites, including ancient ball courts.

forced the Hohokam people to leave. And there's another theory that 100 to 200 years of successive droughts, peaking between 1276 and 1299, brought about the Hohokam's decline.

Into the Ruins

The ranger led a group of us, perhaps twenty tourists, to Casa Grande (Big House), so named by Father Eusebio Francisco Kino. Now sheltered by an enormous modern roof-structure, Casa Grande was constructed of

Robert J. Smith

Astral Chronometer.
Did the Hohokam use astronomical observation to determine agricultural planting cycles? The holes in the ruin's walls may have been aligned with the movements of stars for this purpose.

Buddy Mays

Happy Trails.
The cowboy is the quintessential Western folk hero as well as a real-life citizen of the range.

high-lime-content caliche earth and is the size of a large two- or three-story house. The edifice may have been a residence, storage facility, temple or palace, administrative center, or observatory for stargazers; no one really knows. It stands mysteriously, evocative of Aztec or Mayan structures because of its shape, the ball courts, and the holes in the walls.

The holes in some of the upper walls at Casa Grande may have been oriented toward celestial movements, much like openings in the dome of the astronomical observatory at Chichén Itzá, the Mayan city on Mexico's Yucatan Peninsula.

Astronomical observations may have triggered the Hohokams' planting cycles. Their diet was based on beans, maize, and squash, with additional food harvested from the desert. The saguaro cactus was a mainstay; they ate the fruit, made wine and vinegar from it, and also used the vinegar in etching shells for jewelry. The cactus's ribs were utilized in building construction, and the seeds in tanning hides. Hohokam agriculture was also instrumental in developing trade with distant neighbors.

As we stood on a platform at Casa Grande, overlooking the remnant depressions of ball courts, we talked with a Pima Indian craftswoman. She described imagining the sound of the ball players, like an eerie echo from the past (or a distant roar from a small prehistoric Yankee Stadium). No one knows the significance of these games (just one hard rubber ball has been found in Arizona), but some suggest that religion, rather than pure sport, may have motivated these contests.

As we wandered around Casa Grande, it was dry and dusty, powerful winds blowing across the flatlands. Spirits of the past seemed to shimmer in heat waves over the desert.

Foray into Phoenix

Upon leaving the monument, we followed US 89 to the junction of US 60, then drove eastward toward Apache Junction. We found an RV park by checking *Trailer Life's Campground & RV Services Directory* under the headings *Mesa* and *Apache Junction*. Since it was late spring, the park we chose had plenty of room. Another way to go, especially if you want to catch a glimpse of Mesa, is SR 87 to US 60/89 toward Apache Junction.

We stayed at the View Point and thoroughly enjoyed the luxury of the swimming pool, telephones, and concrete pull-throughs, despite our commitment to the dusty rigors of backroad RVing.

The Phoenix Zoo

Our Phoenix tour began in the morning driving on University Avenue, which we decided was the long way into town . . . so many stoplights! At Apache Boulevard (or US 60/89), which becomes Van Buren, we followed our maps and located the entrance to the Phoenix Zoo (free parking). Safari Trains are available to shuttle visitors around the 125 acres of the country's largest, nonprofit, nontax-supported zoo. We walked around the curving roads delighting in some of the 1,200 mammals that reside in spacious habitats. Munching on hot dogs and watching some ducks squabbling, we wandered on past lounging leopards, drinking elephants, and grazing giraffes and zebras. It was a fine, sunny morning.

Of special note for zoo visitors are the Children's Zoo, the Arizona Exhibit, and a herd of rare Arabian oryx (also, next to the zoo are the enormous Papago Park and Papago Municipal Golf Course).

City Museums

Next we found our way to the Pueblo Grande Museum, at 4619 East Washington Street, where a self-guided tour leads to a site overlooking the remains of Hohokam dwellings. Pueblo Grande represents one of many big Hohokam sites near the remains of their vast network in the Salt River Valley. It's quite amazing to view this archaeological relic surrounded by a bustling metropolitan area, the past miraculously intact despite many intervening centuries.

Our next stop was the Heard Museum, located off Central Avenue on 22 East Monte Vista Road. A must-see, the Heard is a museum of anthropology and primitive arts, presenting an incomparable perspective on

Southwestern Showcase.
(Above) More than 75,000 artifacts fill the Heard Museum's marvelous collections, including these Mojave figurines. *(Below)* Arched walkways of the Heard Museum welcome visitors.

Arts of Past and Present.
The Heard Museum introduces visitors to the lifeways of Native Americans and non-Western societies. Contemporary and traditional work is shown. Pictured is Nora Naranjo Morse's sculpture, *Pearlene.*

the past and present of southwestern Indian cultures, and sometimes those of South America, Asia, and Africa as well. The Heard's stellar collection, "Native Peoples of the Southwest," includes exhibits of ceramics from before the time of Christ to the height of the Hohokam culture between A.D. 1000 and A.D. 1400, all the way to the nineteenth and twentieth centuries.

The Heard, founded by Phoenix pioneers Dwight B. and Maie Heard, has a beautiful audiovisual presentation, *Our Voices, Our Land,* and a geographic and climatic orientation display, accompanied by an historic time line from 15,000 B.C. to the present. There are reconstructions of a pit house, Apache wickiup (brush house) and hogan, a marvelous pottery collection, exhibits of jewelry, kachina dolls, blankets, textiles, paintings, art, and sculpture.

The Phoenix Art Museum, at 1625 North Central, displays paintings, sculpture, and decorative arts from the fifteenth through the twentieth centuries. And for those gallery lovers who love to shop and browse, there is Scottsdale, north of Tempe and Mesa, immensely popular as an art center.

Apache Trail Loop

Next day, our trip was a gem: a one-day loop including the renowned Apache Trail, a stronghold of Arizona's beauty. We picked up US 60 to Mesa, then followed Mesa's Main Street (US 60/89) to Apache Junction, the Superstition Mountains beckoning to the east. Apache Trail is a popular RV area. Part of the road is dirt, and some of it is narrow, but experienced RVers have attested to its navigability in a motorhome smaller than twenty-five feet. Luckily, we had the use of a truck, and the trip was decidedly worth any minor hardships.

Boyce Thompson Southwestern Arboretum

At Florence Junction, we picked up US 60, driving three miles west of Superior to the Boyce Thompson Southwestern Aboretum envisioned in the 1920s by William Boyce Thompson, a mining tycoon who believed in the possibility of eliminating hunger and privation through plant products. The facility is dedicated to plant research and serves as a field museum for the University of Arizona. Thirty-five diversely planted acres are threaded by paths that border streams, climb through rocks, and meander under shadowy overhanging boughs.

The Apache Trail to Roosevelt Lake

After passing through Superior on US 60, we began the ascent toward Globe; at the outskirts we turned off onto SR 88, the Apache Trail, still

Apache Trail.
Twenty-eight rugged miles make up the dirt section of the scenic backroad, the Apache Trail. Here, yellow Palo Verde flowers blaze against a rocky backdrop.

Robert J. Smith

Robert J. Smith

Intrepid RVer.
Some brave souls might take a trailer over the entire length of the Apache Trail. Perhaps, more advisable would be unhooking the trailer and going the distance in the car alone. Fish Creek Hill is a tight squeeze in several spots.

paved at this point. From there, a thirty-one-mile drive brought us to a vista of Theodore Roosevelt Lake, inset like a massive lapis lazuli in the earth. Overlooking the lake is the Tonto National Monument, another impressive historical treasure preserved under government custody. Roosevelt Lake was formed when Roosevelt Dam was built in 1911 on the Salt River. The lake, a bonanza for boating and largemouth bass fishing has probably obscured invaluable artifacts of the Salado (Spanish for "salt") culture, whose members grew a wide variety of vegetables and produced a distinctive pottery called Gila polychrome.

Tonto National Monument

At Tonto National Monument, we parked, walked up to the monument building, and flashed our National Park Golden Eagle Passport. The card costs $25 (at any national park) and provides the pass holder and any accompanying passengers unlimited admission to national parks and monuments for a year. We toured the museum display and saw a film describing the Salado people.

Salado Culture.
Tonto National Monument is the primary site for study of the Salado Indian culture. These cave houses provided more defensible dwellings than those of their Hohokam neighbors.

This group, whose migrations began in north-central Arizona and led southward to the Gila and Salt rivers, was most vital between A.D. 1100 and A.D. 1300 (declining by 1400). The Salado people formed a society that meshed elements of the three major southwestern Indian cultures: the Hohokam, Anasazi, and Mogollon (muggy•youn) groups. There is some evidence that the Salado people lived peacefully and traded with the Hohokam.

A noted cultural anthropologist we spoke to believes the Salado were an "amalgam" Indian group in western New Mexico and Arizona, on the fringe of the Hohokam, Anasazi, and Mogollon cultures. However, we were astounded by examples of the Salados' fine, complex cotton weaving as well as by their jewelry and distinctive pottery. It's clear they mastered many aspects of a difficult desert environment, using its plants and animals to provide a remarkably full life beyond the necessities of mere survival.

They appear to have constructed the monument's three Salado cliff villages (about seventy-two rooms in all) as a defensive measure against their adversaries. The uphill hike (a forty-five-minute round trip) to the primary ruin may be a tough climb for some, but the dwelling, tucked in under an overhang, is interesting, and the view is superb. The Salado people have left an undeniable presence in the hills and terrain of the Tonto National Forest.

The Roosevelt Dam Area

From the monument, we drove over to Roosevelt Dam, whose construction was encouraged by Theodore Roosevelt under the Reclamation Act of 1902. Hand-cut stones were used, and it is said that the dam is the biggest macadam structure in the United States.

Liquid Sky.
Theodore Roosevelt Lake, twenty-five miles long, was created by Roosevelt Dam, which is 275 feet high. Many recreational opportunities were made possible by this first federal reclamation project.

Robert J. Smith

Buddy Mays

Ride the Back Country.
The ultimate backroad wandering may be on horses over wilderness trails. The Superstition Mountains are a favorite place for equestrians.

Next, we plunged into the roller coaster of the Apache Trail's dirt section, noting the signs at the start about certain areas (including Roosevelt Dam) being off limits to vehicles over thirty feet long. We were glad to be driving a truck on the tricky twenty-eight-mile road with its maximum speeds of twenty to thirty miles an hour. This kinky, curvy, sometimes one-lane highway, exhilarating to drive in a truck, would probably be hair-raising in a large motorhome. A small one would have no problem, but there are hairpin curves and the washboard surface of this part of the trail will certainly provide a thoroughly bumpy ride.

But it's worth it! There are vistas, rock formations, glimpses of shimmering green lakes, and mountains: the Superstitions, the Mazatzals, and Sierra Anchas. Those emerald impoundments are the Salt River Chain of Lakes, a magnificent strand including Saguaro, Canyon, and Apache lakes, the latter rimmed to the north by the 7,645-foot Four Peaks. The Superstition Wilderness is to the south, and the landscape is varied and startling, great dominant rock formations set against clear, blue skies.

Robert J. Smith

RVer's Campsite.
The Superstition Mountains provide a getaway destination for RVers in the Phoenix area. Part of the Tonto National Forest, the Superstitions have numerous primitive sites for the adventurous.

Fish Creek Hill

After Apache Lake we passed through the canyon below Fish Creek Hill, crossed a bridge, and began the ascent up the sometimes one-lane road; it seems but a wide ledge on the canyon wall. There's a marvelous view down on Apache Lake, but this is another area not advisable for large motorhomes. In fact, a note of caution: The entire twenty-eight-mile portion of the Apache Trail between Tortilla Flat and Roosevelt should not be driven in rainy weather or by an inexperienced driver.

Tortilla Flat

The dirt part of the trail ends a few miles before Tortilla Flat, east of Canyon Lake, where a motel, restaurant, and Forest Service campground are available. We saw the weird rock formations responsible for the name

Strand of Sapphires.
The Salt River is the source of four lakes skirted by the Apache Trail. Given the desert surroundings, boating, swimming, water skiing, wind surfing, and fishing are especially fun. From Canyon Lake *(above)* to a desert pool in the Superstitions, aquatic recreation is an integral part of backroads Arizona.

Gold Fever.
"I wanted the gold, and I sought it," wrote Robert Service. This might have been the motto of one Jacob Waltz, famous namesake of the Lost Dutchman State Park. His allegedly fabulous gold find in the Superstition Mountains was forever lost.

supplied by boundary commissioner Major William Emory who, in 1853, commented on the "flat tortillas that resemble mountains." Canyon and Apache lakes are recreational playgrounds with boating, waterskiing, and fishing. Hikers, hunters, backpackers, and would-be gold miners are devotees of the area.

Apache Junction

As we neared Apache Junction, we passed Lost Dutchman State Park, named for the legendary gold mine of the German prospector, Jacob Waltz, the "Dutchman" who claimed he'd hit the jackpot in the Superstition Mountains. Whether the mine really existed is unknown; many have died in search of it. With the Superstitions' rocky backdrop, the state park is a scenic place to camp and offers a departure point for hikers and equestrians venturing into the mountains. Five miles from the park lies Apache Junction, the commercial center for this recreational area. We took pictures of the mountains, then gratefully returned to our base at Mesa's outskirts and a swim in the campground's pool.

POINTS OF INTEREST: Arizona Tour 4

The Phoenix Circle

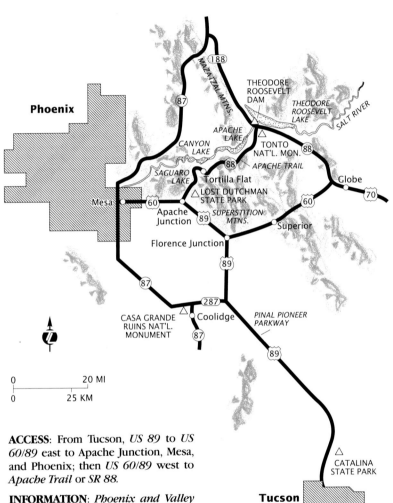

ACCESS: From Tucson, *US 89 to US 60/89* east to Apache Junction, Mesa, and Phoenix; then *US 60/89* west to *Apache Trail* or *SR 88*.

INFORMATION: *Phoenix and Valley of the Sun Convention and Visitors Bureau*, 505 N. 2nd St., Ste. 300, Phoenix 85004-3998 (602) 254-6500; *Mesa Convention and Visitors Bureau*, 120 N. Center, Mesa 85201 (602) 969-1307, (800) 283-MESA; *Apache Junction Chamber of Commerce*, 1001 N. Idaho Rd., P.O. Box 1747, Apache Junction 85217 (602) 982-3141.

ANNUAL EVENTS:

Tempe: *Old Town Tempe Festival of the Arts* (one of the top ten in the country), spring and fall.

Phoenix: *Park-N-Swap*, Phoenix Greyhound Park, Friday–Sunday year-round; *Phoenix Civic Plaza* (changing musical concerts from pop to semi-classical), *Annual Arizona Boat Show*, (602) 967-8714, January.

Apache Junction: *Park-N-Swap*, Apache Greyhound Park, Thursday–Sunday year-round; *Lost Dutchman Days* (concerts, rodeo, carnival, parade), February.

Casa Grande: *O'Odham Tash* (gathering of 100,000–150,000 Indians and Anglos for three-day celebration and all-Indian rodeo), (602) 836-4723, February.

MUSEUMS AND GALLERIES:

Phoenix: *The Heard Museum*, (602) 252-8840; *Phoenix Art Museum*, (602) 257-1222; *Pueblo Grande Museum*, (602) 255-4470; *Arizona Historical Society Museum*, (602) 255-4470.

SPECIAL ATTRACTIONS:

Phoenix: *Turf Paradise* (horse racing), 1501 W. Bell Rd., (602) 942-1101, October–May; first post 1 P.M.

NEARBY ATTRACTIONS:

Casa Grande National Monument, one mile north of Coolidge on SR 87, almost halfway between Phoenix and Tucson, daily 7 A.M.–6 P.M.; *Gila Indian Crafts Center*, thirty miles south of Phoenix on I-10 at Exit 175, junction of SR 93 and I-10, fifteen miles south of Chandler; daily 9 A.M.–5 P.M.

COOL MOUNTAIN HEIGHTS
Along the Mogollon Rim

*In mid-February of 1882, I rode into Prescott
on a long-legged, dapple grey mare who had just
left her footprints the full length of the Santa Fe
trail. We had been three months coming—three
winter months with covered wagons and a
caravan of loose horses—like Abraham and his
family seeking new grazing grounds.*

Sharlot M. Hall,
Sharlot Hall on the Arizona Strip

T he following day we set out toward the mining towns of Miami and Globe on US 89/60, initially retracing the previous day's path. The mountainous regions above the Mogollon Rim were beckoning with a change of climate and forested heights.

Globe got its name from the discovery of a globe-shaped, fifty-pound, almost-pure silver nugget. From this mining town, you can take US 70 southwest to San Carlos Lake on the San Carlos Indian Reservation (the reservation's borders start just outside of Globe).

San Carlos Apache Indian Reservation

There are actually two reservations side by side: the Fort Apache Reservation taking up approximately the northern half of the total area, the San Carlos to the south. The boundary between the two is the Black River (to the east); it joins the White River, forming the Salt River, for the western boundary.

San Carlos covers 1,853,841 acres, the state's fourth-largest reservation. Its southern zone is made up of desert highlands, cacti, and desert trees; the central zone by grassy mountain ridges; and the northeastern by forests of ponderosa pine, blue spruce, and aspen trees. The reservation is a paradise for anglers and hunters, and these activities are governed by the Apaches. As the reservation brochure explains, the "appropriate Reservation licenses, tags and permits . . . may be obtained at Tribal Headquarters in San Carlos or at Soda Canyon Store in San Carlos Lake."

There are developed campgrounds open to the public on the reservation and marked on the brochure's map. Fishing in San Carlos, as in Roosevelt Lake, is for largemouth bass, crappie, and catfish. Other fishing possibilities include Phillips Park Lake, one of several trout lakes on the reservation. For hunters there are deer, elk, javelina, quail, and turkey.

The brochure justly forewarns visitors to come prepared since much of the reservation is primitive, undeveloped country and roads occasionally become impassable; taking a truck into remote areas is advisable.

A few years before we'd fished for Apache trout (a unique strain, more like cutthroat than rainbow trout) in the Black River, but this time we didn't stop, heading northeast through the reservation on SR 77/US 60 to Show Low (which lies just beyond the Fort Apache Reservation border).

The Salt River Canyon

The ninety-mile drive from Globe to Show Low took us through panoramic country, especially the Salt River Canyon, a junior version of the Grand Canyon. US 60 provides a 2,000-foot descent in five miles via massive switchbacks, but using lower gears, we felt entirely secure on the

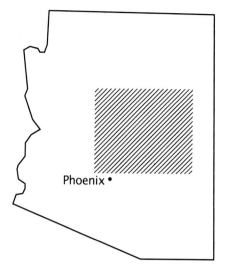

Phoenix •

Tour **5** *366 miles*

SAN CARLOS APACHE INDIAN RESERVATION • FORT APACHE INDIAN RESERVATION • SHOW LOW • CAMP VERDE • MONTEZUMA CASTLE NATIONAL MONUMENT • SEDONA • TUZIGOOT NATIONAL MONUMENT • JEROME • PRESCOTT • ARCOSANTI

Slick Rock Cliffs.
Slick rock cliffs, such as these near Sedona, were favorite buildings spots for the Anasazi because of the protection they offered.

Mountain Hideaway.
RVers and Arizonans alike seek out the White Mountains for cooler environs and campsites like this one.

Robert J. Smith

sweeping curves. Observing the colorful rock formations from several turnouts, at the bottom we crossed the bridge, and began the five-mile ascent back out.

Fort Apache Indian Reservation

The Salt River Bridge marks the beginning of the Fort Apache Reservation, home of the White Mountain Apaches, an enterprising people utilizing their resources in lumber, cattle operations, and recreation. Their section

Robert J. Smith

Salt River Canyon.
The best part of Salt River Canyon is the road that spirals down into and out of it (descending 2,000 feet in five miles). Travelers can picnic by the bridge across the Salt River.

of the White Mountains has 1,664,872 acres, the reservation's northern edge butting up against the Mogollon Rim. The Apaches maintain some twenty-six lakes for trout fishing, over 300 miles of trout streams, campsites for tents and RVs, and ski runs at the Apache Sunrise Ski Resort. For hunters, there is everything from quail to elk. In fact, the largest trophy elk in the nation come from White Mountain Apache lands. The management of all these recreational opportunities is handled by the White Mountain Apache Recreation Enterprise.

White Mountains and Environs

Coming from the flatlands, we ascended into the White Mountains, to the Mogollon Rim. With the gain in altitude, there are spruce, juniper, and ponderosa pine, a cooling of the air, and a soothing of the soul in blue-green vistas.

Instead of going straight to Show Low, another point of access to the White Mountains is via SR 73; it heads southeast to Fort Apache, then north to Whiteriver. Now a museum and once the military quarters used by General George Crook and his soldiers, Fort Apache was built at a

crucial junction betwen the Navajo tribes to the north and the Apache Indians to the south, perhaps the most famed outpost of United States forces during the Indian campaigns.

Crook built a road between Fort Apache and Camp Verde to the west after a 700-mile ramble by mule in Arizona's mountains. Following the Mogollon Rim for 200 miles, the road, which can still be seen, provided a vital link for transfer of supplies and information during Crook's 1872–1873 campaign that ended the Indian wars. A few days later, we paralleled the same route from the Fort Apache area to Camp Verde and Prescott.

Whiteriver, north of Fort Apache on SR 73, is the Apache tribal capital and contains a trading post. We drove west on SR 260 toward Show Low to meet with a friend of ours for some fishing.

The Show Low Area

In Show Low, we met up with Sam Knoy, a native Arizonan friend from Prescott; we were going to fish for Apache trout in the White Mountains. Based at one of the local RV parks in Show Low, we visited the Federal Fish Hatchery at Hon Dah and obtained a boating permit at Pinetop. We'd already received our fishing permits by mail from the White Mountain Apache Tribe. Reservation visitors are subject to Apache Nation laws, and poaching is a fined offense. Several lakes have special seasons and license requirements, so it's advisable to get details from the White Mountain Apache Recreation Enterprise, P.O. Box 220, Whiteriver, Arizona 85941, (602) 338-4385.

Show Low is an all-American small town, an oasis for people from sweltering Phoenix who come for the greenery, cool nights, and dry, hot days in summertime. Other famous towns in the region include Pinetop, Lakeside, and Springerville.

We appreciated the change of scenery and were entertained by the story behind Show Low's name. In 1875, there were two neighbors living in close proximity, a fellow named Marion Clark, and Corydon E. Cooley, a scout for Crook in the Apache wars (Cooley had two wives, daughters of a local chief). One day the men agreed that claustrophobia had set in and someone had to move away. The situation was to be settled by playing cards. Clark said, "If you can show low, you win." Cooley drew the deuce of clubs. "Show low it is." And so we have Show Low, Arizona, also known now as the "Gateway to the White Mountains." The main street also honors the card game with its name, "Deuce of Clubs."

The next day we traveled about an hour on a well-maintained dirt road, and launched Sam's little car-top boat (powered by an electric trolling motor) in a specially managed lake. Using both wet and dry flies, we caught several sixteen-inch brown and Apache trout, but decided that

Buddy Mays

Apache Sentinels.
Saguaro cacti stud the hills of the San Carlos Apache Indian Reservation.

Gone Fishin'.
The Black River is a well-known source of Apache trout and smallmouth bass. Accessible from the northern edge of the San Carlos Indian Reservation, it takes a rugged trek to reach the river canyon.

while each of us was allowed to keep two Apache trout, we'd release the fish back in the lake, doing our part for Apache restocking efforts (this species once native to Arizona). We let go the majority of brown trout, too, but kept a few to eat. There's nothing like a delicious lakeside lunch of campfire-grilled brown trout, skillet-fried onions with potatoes, and a tomato-cucumber salad.

Later in the afternoon, we met a very courteous Apache game warden and thoroughly enjoyed an hour's conversation about his culture and customs. Only one of his three children speaks Apache; his most difficult task as a father and Apache is keeping the culture alive. The warden spoke Navajo (which has similar linguistic roots, but a completely different dialect), Apache, Spanish, and English. We found it interesting that he'd given up big-game hunting with a rifle but still enjoys hunting and stalking game with an old-fashioned bow and arrow.

Along the Mogollon Rim

Next day, we made our way along picturesque SR 260, admiring panoramas of the forested world below. The Mogollon Rim is a 200-mile precipitous escarpment (also called the "backbone of Arizona"), separating Arizona's high country from the lowlands. We stopped the motorhome several times to take pictures.

There's a turnoff to SR 260 and Zane Grey's cabin, but we don't advise taking this trip; a rough paved road turns into dirt and hairpin curves. At the dead end, where the cabin is situated, there's no room to manuever or turn around a large trailer or motorhome.

Onward to Camp Verde

Camp Verde was that night's destination, and we drove on through Payson, another favorite summer oasis for Phoenix residents who want to escape the heat. Each September, Payson fills with contestants and fiddle-music lovers for the Old Time Fiddlers Contest. The road passes Strawberry, where the state's oldest schoolhouse, built in 1887, still stands. Then it was east on the paved Zane Grey Highway, thirty-four miles to Camp Verde.

The Verde River, life force of the Verde Valley, has long been a reliable water source, the foundation of numerous settlements for hundreds, if not thousands, of years. The Sinagua, Hohokam, Yavapai, Tonto Apaches, and finally, Anglo-European immigrants have all left their marks in this part of Arizona.

During the 1860s, Arizona Volunteers built Camp Verde (then Camp Lincoln) to defend settlers in the valley from raiding Apache Indians. The fort was renamed Fort Verde by the U.S. Army and used as a base for General Crook in 1872 and 1873. Vigilant and persistent during a "pacification" campaign that ranged from the Superstition Mountains to the Mogollon Rim, Crook's soldiers and Indian scouts were described by one officer in this way: "A dirtier, greasier, more uncouth looking set of of-

Floral Finery.
The hedgehog cactus graces the harsh desert terrain.

Roger and Donna Aitkenhead

ficers and men it would be hard to encounter anywhere. . . . " But Camp Verde in its day was considered to be an oasis of civilization, complete with lace curtains, well-dressed women, and officers in smart uniforms. Compared to some of the other forts, life was carried on with élan.

Today, there are four buildings in the ten-acre Fort Verde State Historic Park where Crook accepted the surrender of the Apache chief Cha-lipun and 300 of his warriors. A museum displays military uniforms, firearms, and memorabilia of the period; a modest admission fee is charged.

Montezuma Castle National Monument

We spent the night in Camp Verde, and next day followed the sign to Montezuma Castle National Monument, five miles north. After parking our rig, we walked the quarter-mile pathway to view the 900-year-old "castle," the well-defended cliff residence of about fifty members of the Sinagua group. Its construction was completed in the thirteenth century, a time when drought had brought social upheaval to the Southwest. The five-story structure, built into a limestone cliff overlooking Verde Valley's Beaver Creek, is too fragile to be entered. Half a million visitors a year see this relic of the Sinagua, who also lived around what is now Flagstaff.

Cliff Castle.
The silent ruin called Montezuma Castle was once a five-story, prehistoric cliff dwelling, accessible only by ladders. Nearby Beaver Creek provided the inhabitants with water.

Robert J. Smith

Robert J. Smith

Spring-fed Pool.
Montezuma Well has been a water source for centuries, an oasis attracting settlement and agricultural development.

According to archaeologists, the Hohokam inhabited the area first, about A.D. 600, living in pit houses near Beaver Creek. Next came the Sinagua (Spanish for "without water"), dry-land farmers who arrived from the vicinity of Flagstaff around A.D. 1125. The two groups seem to have intermingled without conflict, pooling their knowledge, talent, and survival skills for the benefit of both groups.

Montezuma Well, a detached portion of the monument, is about eleven miles northeast. This limestone sinkhole, 470 feet wide and 55 feet deep, is rimmed by cliff dwellings and pueblos. Sinagua farmers who lived there utilized the sinkhole to irrigate their crops in the valley.

The Glorious Road to Sedona

From Montezuma Well, we continued north on I-17, taking the exit to SR 179 and then US 89A, the scenic two-lane highway that leads to Sedona and famed Oak Creek Canyon. It's like driving through a post card; the

Summer Country.
Oak Creek is a haven for campers and funlovers. Combined with the red buttes and Sedona's many restaurants and art galleries, the area is a playground paradise. Oak Creek Canyon is known as "the Grand Canyon with a road."

Buddy Mays

Sedona Sandstone.
Slick rock is the term used for the red sandstone bluffs found in Oak Creek Canyon.

The Cowboy Artists of America were formed in Sedona in 1965 by George Phippen, Charlie Dye, John Hampton, and Joe Beeler. Their goal is to "perpetuate the memory and culture of the Old West . . . to insure authentic representation of the life of the West as it was and is."

country is a bastion of rock formations, monolithic red-rock buttes and cliffs studding the juniper and ponderosa-forested landscape. Inset within this natural grandeur is the town of Sedona, a center for traditional and contemporary arts.

Art galleries and restaurants are found throughout the city; one of the most famous complexes is Tlaquepaque, a replica of the suburb of Guadalajara, Mexico, where the mazelike adobe buildings contain a treasure trove of galleries, shops, and restaurants. One of Sedona's best galleries is the Elaine Horwitch Art Gallery, noted for its imaginative work by a variety of artists (not in the Tlaquepaque complex).

For a complete change of pace, there's Oak Creek Canyon near town, a favorite spot for swimming, bodysurfing, tubing down Slide Rock, and camping.

We were in Sedona on Memorial Day weekend and found it necessary to camp in a vacant lot in town, so full were the campgrounds. Sedona has become extremely popular and is often filled with tourists. Nevertheless, the drive and the town are worth a visit, even on a busy holiday.

Buddy Mays

Rock Climber's Delight.
Sedona's extensive rock formations provide a perfect setting for exploration.

Tuzigoot National Monument

After our night in the parking lot, we set out southwest on US 89A through Cottonwood toward the Tuzigoot National Monument. (The turnoff for Tuzigoot is between Cottonwood and Clarkdale.) If we'd been smarter the night before, we'd have stayed in Cottonwood at the Dead Horse Ranch State Park, which has campsites and hookups. The wind was blowing hard as we walked around the 100-room pueblo, a Sinagua structure erected primarily in the 1200s atop a 120-foot-high ridge. The Verde Valley and Verde River are clearly visible from the vantage point of the now-roofless pueblo. We thoroughly enjoyed the museum at the monument, one of the best we visited.

Archaic Lookout.
Tuzigoot, Apache for "crooked water," is located on top of a 120-foot-high ridge in the Verde Valley. A center for ancient farmers, the original fifteen to twenty rooms expanded to ninety-two rooms as the population grew.

Buddy Mays

Jerome State Historic Park

Our next stop, Jerome, was formerly a booming mining town. When the United Verde Branch copper mines of the Phelps Dodge Corporation closed in 1953, it became a virtual ghost town. Rescued from its decline (and some of it *was* literally sliding downhill), Jerome's serpentine streets are now lined with art galleries, restaurants, shops, and museums. The narrow streets are almost impossible to navigate with a long rig, but there are several parking areas and turnouts before entering town.

Jerome State Historic Park is off US 89A and open daily from 8:00 A.M. to 5:00 P.M. The park museum is located in the old Douglas Mansion and traces the history of local mining and the family of James S. Douglas, developer of the United Verde Extension in the early 1900s.

Prescott Gold Mining Country

From Jerome, US 89A, the backroad to Prescott, travels over 7,743-foot-high Mingus Mountain. We drove about twenty-five miles to the intersection with US 89, then another five miles to Prescott, where we stayed at the Point of Rocks Campground in the Granite Dells. The view from the Dells is a compelling, 360-degree view of the high desert landscape around historic Prescott, twice the capital of the Arizona Territory. This is the gold mining country that drew explorer and mountain man Joseph Walker and his group of miners to dangerous Indian lands in 1863. Overland pioneers following Walker's footsteps made comments on their arduous land journey that can only fill an RVer's heart with gratitude:

> A man must be able to endure heat like a salamander, mud and water like a muskrat, dust like a toad, labor like a jackass.
>   Road very bad, teams gave out.
>   Oh, the mosquitoes.

Early-day Prescott was a wild frontier town. When its first hotel opened on July 4, 1864, the menu for breakfast was fried venison and chili; for lunch, chili baked beans and chili on tortillas; and for supper, chili. In the last quarter of the nineteenth century, infamous Whiskey Row on Montezuma Street provided recreation. The few bars here now merely hint at the "good old days" when drinking, fighting, gambling, and other diverting activities took the edge off the hard life of ranchers and miners. On the night of July 14, 1900, Whiskey Row burned to the ground, and as local citizens readied themselves to rebuild, a group sang the Rough Rider favorite, "There'll Be a Hot Time in the Old Town Tonight."

Prescott has long been known as a cool, piney refuge from the brutally hot summers in Phoenix. The town has character, from the old Courthouse Building in the central square with its statue of Bucky O'Neill, the first volunteer in the Spanish-American War and organizer of the Rough Riders, to the July Fourth Frontier Days Celebration and Rodeo, featuring a parade, fireworks, and the world's oldest rodeo. Although congested and growing, Prescott fills a particular niche in Arizona's history. Prescott townspeople are dedicated to preserving the past in a variety of ways. Antique stores seem to be everywhere, and there are a number of good restaurants, too, with interiors evocative of times past.

We enjoyed a delicious dinner at one of Prescott's favorite restaurants, Murphy's, located in a historic 1890 mercantile building at 201 North Cortez Street. The wood-paneled interior, replacing the cavernous spaces of the old store, has been fully restored to depict the era. The specialities of the house are mesquite-broiled seafood and freshly baked breads.

A famous landmark at 122 East Gurley Street is the Hassayampa Inn, a community project financed by the sale of stock to Prescottonians and opened in 1927. Restored in 1985, the intricate mural on its lobby ceiling is still a bright work of art. The Hassayampa, at one time the town's pride and joy, is now listed on the National Register of Historic Places and features the Peacock Room restaurant as well as guest accommodations.

The Rough Riders was the nickname of the 1st Regiment of U.S. Cavalry Volunteers. Bucky O'Neill was the first of the western ranchers and cowboys who comprised most of the members of the famed adventurers, organized by Theodore Roosevelt to help fight the Spanish-American War in 1898.

Prescott's Pride.
This all-American hometown was built by mining and ranching interests. The cattle industry is still a strong one locally, and horse riding is not only a favorite pastime, but a working necessity. Surrounded by the Prescott National Forest, Prescottonians have miles of wilderness to explore on horseback.

Buddy Mays

Arcosanti

Energy Efficient.
Paolo Soleri's visionary concept of architecture and ecology that work in harmony seem now, more than ever, a necessity. Arcosanti is the kind of daring experiment made possible by Arizona's perfect weather and creative climate. *Newsweek* magazine reported that "as urban architecture, Arcosanti is probably the most important experiment undertaken in our lifetime."

Arcosanti

Our last stop on this varied and delightful ramble was Arcosanti, the unfinished solar energy dream city of visionary architect and urban planner Paolo Soleri; it stands approximately one mile north of Cordes Junction. The as-yet-unfinished twenty-five-story vertical city was conceived by Soleri as an alternative to uncontrolled urban growth. The completed project will encompass a fifteen-acre area with living and working accommodations for about 5,000 inhabitants.

Curious to see the revolutionary structure, we made the pilgrimage. It reminded us of a futuristic Anasazi dwelling (lest we forget that the Southwest's prehistoric inhabitants were attuned not only to vertical cities, but also to passive solar energy). A modest donation is charged, and there are hourly tours. The word *Arcosanti* comes from *arcology* (from architecture and ecology) and *cosanti* (Italian for *before things*). Cosanti is also the name of Soleri's studio in Scottsdale, which is also open to visitors. We thoroughly enjoyed our visit to one man's dream of a better future for humanity.

POINTS OF INTEREST: Arizona Tour 5

Along the Mogollon Rim

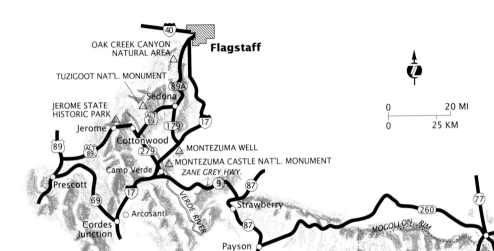

ACCESS: From Apache Junction to *US 60* north.

INFORMATION: *Arcosanti*, I-17 at Cordes Junction, Mayer 86333 (602) 632-7135; *Globe/Miami Chamber of Commerce*, 1450 N. Broad St., Globe 85501 (602) 425-4495; *Show Low Chamber of Commerce*, 951 W. Deuce of Clubs, P.O. Box 1083, Show Low 85901 (602) 537-2326; *Alpine Chamber of Commerce*, P.O. Box 410, Alpine 85920; *Camp Verde Chamber of Commerce*, Journal Office, Main St. and Turner, P.O. Box 1665, Camp Verde 86322 (602) 567-3341; *Sedona-Oak Creek Canyon Chamber of Commerce*, Corner 89A and Forest Rd., P.O. Box 478, Sedona 86336 (602) 282-7722; *Jerome Chamber of Commerce*, Drawer K, P.O. 788, Jerome 86331 (602) 634-5716; *Prescott Chamber of Commerce*, 117 W. Goodwin St., P.O. Box 1147, Prescott 86302 (602) 445-2000.

ANNUAL EVENTS:

Whiteriver: *Mountain Days Celebration Rodeo*, July.

Prescott: *Frontier Days and World's Oldest Rodeo*, July.

Show Low: *Fourth of July Celebration* (parade, rodeo, fireworks); *Show Low Shootout* (cavalry re-enactments, arts and crafts, entertainment), October.

MUSEUMS AND GALLERIES:

Prescott: *Sharlot Hall Museum*, 415 W. Gurley, (602) 445-3122; *Smoki Museum*, 100 N. Arizona, (602) 445-9840.

RESTAURANTS:

Prescott: *Murphy*'s, Cortez St., (602) 445-4044; *Peacock Room*, (602) 778-9434, the *Hassayampa Inn*, Gurley and Marina streets, Prescott.

METEORS AND VOLCANOES
Grand Canyon Country

Now the firmament is bounded only by the horizon, and what a vast expanse of constellations can be seen! The river rolls by us in silent majesty; the quiet of the camp is sweet; our joy is ecstasy. We sit till long after midnight talking of the Grand Canyon, talking of home.

Major John Wesley Powell,
writing in his journal

Buddy Mays

86

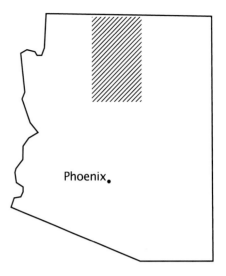

Flagstaff was our base of operations for an exploration of north-central Arizona. The area around "Flag" is alpine, high desert, and mountainous—entirely different from the desert to the south. Many recreational vehicle parks are available, and we chose one centrally located and easily accessible to stores and malls. There were numerous sights to see in the immediate area before our trip to the Grand Canyon.

Exploring the Flagstaff Area

Meteor Crater

We drove thirty-five miles on I-40 east of Flagstaff to Meteor Crater, the best preserved on earth, designated a natural landmark in 1968 by the Department of the Interior. The 570-foot-deep crater is out on the plains west of Winslow. Approaching it on Meteor Crater Road, we felt a sense of excitement about witnessing the place where outer space's calling card fell to earth. Smashing into the planet 30,000 years ago, the nickel-iron meteorite was 80 to 100 feet in diameter, traveling at 43,000 miles per hour. Eighty percent of its volume vaporized on impact, five percent was physically ejected from the crater, and ten percent is still buried at the crater's south rim. The impact must have been devastating!

As it rammed the earth, a mushroom-shaped cloud billowed into the stratosphere releasing shrapnel of nickel-iron and rock pellets that hurtled downward on trees, animals, and terrain. Hard as it is to imagine this event, scientists have calculated that 300 million tons of rock were displaced, the majority of this material creating the uplifted rim of the crater.

The crater is used in the training of astronauts and in space exploration studies. (NASA trained the *Apollo* astronauts here.) There's a small museum where films are shown and lectures given. There is also an RV park just five miles from the attraction. For hours and fee information, call the Meteor Crater Museum at (602) 526-5259, and the RV Park at (602) 289-4002.

Walnut Canyon National Monument

After the crater, we returned to Flagstaff, stopping at Walnut Canyon National Monument at the end of a three-mile road off I-40, about 7½ miles east of Flagstaff. As early as A.D. 600, the canyon, 400 feet deep, was the home of Sinagua Indians. Their 300 dwellings, built under the overhanging cliffs, testify to a flourishing settlement here between A.D. 1125 and A.D. 1250. The Sinagua farmed the fertile soil on the rim, using check dams and terraces to conserve available water runoff. They also foraged from nature's garden for wild grape, serviceberry, elderberry, yucca, and Arizona black walnut.

Prehistoric Picture Window.
Canyon-dwelling Indians may once have called this tiny ruin home; however, scientists are still unsure whether the Nankoweap ruins were actually dwellings or merely used as storage cysts for corn or other agricultural products.

Tour **6** *440 miles*

METEOR CRATER • WALNUT CANYON NATIONAL MONUMENT • SUNSET CRATER NATIONAL MONUMENT • WUPATKI NATIONAL MONUMENT • FLAGSTAFF • GRAND CANYON NATIONAL PARK

The monument, at 7,000 feet, covers 2,249 acres. Visitors with heart problems may wish to avoid the steep three-quarter-mile round-trip tour into the canyon. There's a shorter, easier trail along the canyon rim for those who don't like to climb. A museum and brochure describe the life of the Sinagua and their active trading with other peoples.

Sunset Crater National Monument

After viewing Walnut Canyon, we drove north on US 89 to the road into Sunset Crater National Monument, which is on the right, ten miles outside of Flagstaff. The volcanic crater seems to complement the meteor crater, the former created by earth's internal forces, and the latter the result of extraterrestrial impact.

We turned onto the monument road and drove two miles to the visitor center, using our Golden Eagle Passport for admission as we had at other national monuments. There are displays of volcanic rock and a film on volcanoes, and we learned a little about volcanic activity.

Sunset Crater is a 1,000-foot volcanic cone with surrounding formations. The Bonito lava flow, a stark jumble of lava rock, has a mile-long hiking loop. The rangers advised us to wear thick-soled shoes because the lava is sharp. The volcano, which erupted around A.D. 1064, dumped debris upon the Sinagua who lived in the area, forcing them to evacuate their ancestral lands. We read that archaeologists have interpreted the data and concluded that the Sinagua, Anasazi, and Cohonina resettled the area several decades later, constructing the pueblos at the Wupatki National Monument, eighteen miles away from Sunset Crater. The new layer of volcanic ash actually enriched the soil by adding trace elements and trapping moisture, thereby increasing agricultural production for the Indians.

Wupatki National Monument

We continued on the present loop drive past the orange-toned volcanic crater (8,029 feet above sea level) and the somber lava fields, gradually descending to lower elevations and a progressively more dramatic view of the Painted Desert, a large area in the southwest corner of the Navajo Reservation.

The day of our trip was especially magnificent, the sky intensely blue, clouds rolling, the distant Painted Desert a coral pink with gradations of purple and magenta, and the high desert a sea of sage and rust-red rocks. In this fantastic landscape, the ruins at the Wupatki National Monument were a sight to behold, truly one of the high points of our tours.

Among the most impressive of the ruins is Wupatki, or "tall house," with over 100 rooms. Despite the weathered state of the Wupatki and Wukoki ruins (just two of many ancient structures scattered around the

Buddy Mays

Star of the Treetops.
This Stellar Jay makes a home in an oak tree around Flagstaff.

Canyon Condos.
The Sinagua Indians who lived in these small cliffside dwellings subsisted on crops of corn and beans grown in small plots on the canyon rim. The ruins were probably abandoned because of infertile soil by A.D. 1275.

Buddy Mays

Home to Hopi Kachinas.
The San Francisco Peaks, of religious significance to both the Hopi and Navajo, designate the sacred southwest border of Dinetah or Navajoland. They make a dramatic backdrop for ruins at Wupatki National Monument.

area), it takes little imagination to admire the Sinagua and Anasazi Indians who could survive and thrive in the face of the physical obstacles presented by this environment. Nature favored them for a while with a greater level of moisture during the years they were there, and the ash from the volcanic eruption enhanced growth conditions. Yet, the populace had departed by A.D. 1225. Walking around the ruins, we saw the buildings and the ball court (the farthest north in Arizona) at Wupatki, and thought about the untold stories of a prehistoric people, wishing there were definitive answers to our questions: Why had so many of these Indian groups disappeared? Was it due to disease, drought, social upheaval, war, or some cataclysmic disaster? Or was there some other unknown reason?

Flagstaff

The next day was devoted to packing up and taking a short jaunt through Flagstaff's museums. We drove out US 180 to the Pioneers' Historical Museum, noting that what it may lack in displays is made up for in community spirit.

Rick Velotta

Volcanic Cone.
It was in 1064 A.D., just two years before William the Conqueror invaded Britain, that Sunset Crater erupted. An old lava bed can be toured on foot by visitors to Sunset Crater National Monument.

The Museum of Northern Arizona, on the other hand, a little farther on the left, touched upon all we'd learned in our Arizona travels. Galleries are devoted to archaeology, ethnology, geology, biology, and fine arts, including the annual Hopi, Navajo, and Zuni craftspeople's exhibitions in July.

In the courtyard we sat down and ate warm, freshly made pieces of Indian fry bread, prepared by an Indian vendor, and washed the sweet, filling food down with iced tea. Then we returned to town and the last stop on our day trip.

Lowell Observatory

The Lowell Observatory is a treat for anyone interested in astronomy. One mile west of downtown Flagstaff via Santa Fe Avenue, and sequestered in the piney woods on Mars Hill, the old observatory, built in 1894, is still a functioning facility. In fact, it's one of the foremost astronomical observatories in the country. The planet Pluto was discovered from here in 1930. There's a repository for a two-million-photograph collection of the planets.

Robert J. Smith

Touring the Canyon Rims.
RVers are well equipped for the thrilling experience of the Grand Canyon's vistas. The canyon is 277 miles long and at some points 18 miles wide.

Grand Canyon National Park

South Rim

Arizona is known as "the Grand Canyon State," and from Flagstaff, the chasm is about a twenty-eight mile drive on US 180. Admission to the park is by a seven-day ($5) permit. The canyon's spatial dimensions are so immense it's impossible not to feel awe-struck looking down at the seemingly tiny Colorado River below. The Grand Canyon reaches depths of 3½ miles; it was carved by the Colorado River, the elements, and geological upheaval over millions of years. The South Rim offers varying vantage points as one fans out to the east from Grand Canyon Village.

First, there's Yavapai Point, to the west of Mather Point; the Colorado can be seen in a panoramic vista from here. It's also the end of a nature trail that begins at the visitor center at park headquarters. Museums here

Grand Canyon Lookout.
(This page and overleaf) Viewers can observe the effects of erosion caused by snow, rain, and air from any vantage point. The passage of light through the canyon during the course of a day provides a succession of colorful images.

Arizona Office of Tourism

and at Yavapai Point enhance one's appreciation of the Canyon, and a telescope at Yavapai is directed at rock formations. During the season, park rangers give lectures daily at both museums, and there is also a slide show and videotape at Yavapai Point to explain Grand Canyon geology, ecosystems, and habitation.

Tours of the Rim

There are also tours, beyond the simple drive from one vista to the next. Bus tours transport people along the West Rim, a two-hour narrated trip, and along the East Rim, a three-hour journey. Having previously hiked the canyon, we decided simply to drive the rim, but those with an interest in backpacking the Bright Angel or South Kaibab trails should inquire about permits from the Back Country Reservations Office (near Mather Campground). Mule trips are also offered.

Trail Guide.
The greatest trail guide of the canyon was John Hance, a yarnspinner. When asked why his finger was missing, he replied: "I musta wore that thing plumb off pointin' at all the beautiful scenery around here."

Canyon Overview.
The Grand Canyon region incorporates Grand Canyon National Park, national monuments, national forests, Indian reservations and recreation areas. The canyon consists of about 2,000 square miles and a vertical descent of 2,200 feet over its total length.

Architectural Masterpiece.
The Grand Canyon, one of the greatest wonders of the natural world, became a national park in 1918. The perspective from Desert View is spectacular.

Grand Canyon History

The influx of tourists didn't officially begin until 1903, when the Santa Fe Railroad laid down tracks to the South Rim. Prior to that sightseers were transported from Flagstaff and the Williams area via Bright Angel Trail. The earliest Anglo-European tourists were members of Coronado's expedition who came in 1540; the first recorded viewing of the canyon was by Garcia López de Cárdenas, one of the party. The expedition came mainly in search of the Seven Golden Cities of Cibola and an officer, Pedro de Tovar, had been led to believe by Hopis that a fabled river, perhaps the elusive Northwest Passage, was a few days' travel to the west. A descent into the canyon was attempted in pursuit of this possibility, but to no avail.

Over the ensuing centuries other frontierspeople came, such as famed trapper James Ohio Pattie, Lieutenant Amiel Whipple, and a Civil War veteran named John Wesley Powell, who named it the Grand Canyon. Until 1902, Grand Canyon Village was known as Hance's Tank, after trail guide and prospector John Hance, who built the first trail down into the canyon from Bright Angel. He was well known for his tall tales, joining the ranks of those who've made such tongue-in-cheek remarks as: "It'd be a helluva place to lose a cow."

Robert J. Smith

Once again tourists will be able to get to the canyon via railroad. Construction has begun on the Grand Canyon Railway; the first passengers should be able to ride the sixty miles from Williams to the canyon in April, 1990. Historic downtown Williams is sprucing up, too. Part of an $80-million, 1,000-acre development includes refurbishing of the old Harvey Hotel/Fray Marcos, with new guest accommodations and a center with retail shops, restaurants, and visitor services. Phases of the project expected to be completed in the next few years include a theme park and recreation center, new RV park, rodeo arena, Native American cultural complex, ski area, golf course, and another spur for the rail line.

East Rim Drive

The village is also the site of the eighty-year-old El Tovar Hotel and the Hopi House, a reproduction of a Hopi dwelling. These are just starting points for the East Rim Drive, which takes in Yaki Point, with its panoramic crescent view of the canyon; Moran Point, dramatic in the rich light of late afternoon, with a perspective on Hance Rapids, five miles to the northeast; Lipan Point, which reveals the canyon in its greatest

Desert View.
A seventy-foot-high stone watchtower, constructed by the Santa Fe Railroad in 1932, houses a glass-enclosed observation area and powerful telescopes for taking in the panorama.

Robert J. Smith

99

beauty; and a mile east, Navajo Point. There is also Desert View, with its dramatic vantage point, a seventy-foot stone watchtower surveying a ninety-degree turn in the canyon. The tower has a glass-enclosed observatory and powerful telescopes.

Between Desert View and Grand Canyon Village are the remains of a twelfth- and early-thirteenth-century Anasazi village, Tusayan. Because of its location it's the most frequently visited Southwestern ruin. There are campgrounds near Desert View and some outside the park.

After the south and east Grand Canyon rim tours, we drove SR 64 to its junction with US 89, turning north toward Page. Before touring the North Rim, we visited Page and the Glen Canyon Dam.

Page and Glen Canyon

We found ourselves descending to 4,300 feet as we neared Page, a small desert city surrounded by red cliffs and magnificent rock formations. Page was originally planned as the headquarters for workers and officials employed by the Bureau of Reclamation. Now the area is another desert oasis with a huge river impoundment creating many recreational opportunities for boaters, anglers, water-skiers, wind surfers, river rafters, houseboaters and sailors. Page is a pleasant community with many conveniences, a good place to hook up in a local trailer park for a rest after traveling.

Lee's Ferry

South of Page is Lee's Ferry, known for beautiful Vermilion Cliffs, rainbow trout fishing, and for Colorado River whitewater rafting trips. There are also raft trips on the river waters from Glen Canyon Dam to Lee's Ferry, named for an unsavory character—John Doyle Lee, a Mormon who came into the area in 1871. Lee ran a commercial ferry business on the Colorado, but in reality he was running from the law. Before coming to the crossing, Lee made his home in southern Utah not far from the route of California-bound immigrant trains. When a wagon train with some of his Missouri adversaries passed nearby at Mountain Meadows, Paiute Indians were allegedly induced by Lee and other Mormons to attack the wagon train; the battle lasted four days. The Mormons promised safe passage for those who would put down their weapons. But the act of surrender was the signal for betrayal: 140 men, women and children were slaughtered by the Indians and their Mormon comrades and just seventeen youths were allowed to live.

Lee was apprehended by United States marshals in 1874 at Lee's Ferry, but his alibi assigned the blame to Salt Lake City, liberating Lee from responsibility. And perhaps he was a scapegoat in this horrid act of genocide. Nonetheless, he met death before a firing squad at Mountain Meadows, where the massacre had taken place. It wasn't until 1950, with the publication of Juanita Brooks's book, *The Mountain Meadows Massacre,* that Lee was vindicated. Through the efforts of descendants of the ferryman's nineteen wives, after seventy-three years the Mormon Church brought him posthumously back into the fold as a full member in 1961.

Colorado Rainbows.
Fishing in the Colorado is productive for both casual and avid anglers. Some of the largest rainbow trout in America exist in this canyon river.

Buddy Mays

Kaibab Plateau

From Lee's Ferry it's a short drive south to US 89A, and then fifty-five miles to Jacob's Lake and the junction of SR 67, heading south to the North Rim of the Grand Canyon. One of the prettiest drives is the forty-five miles to the North Rim over the Kaibab Plateau. The road travels through thick forest that suddenly opens up into great, green meadows. If you're lucky, you'll see deer and the Kaibab tassel-eared squirrel, a white-tailed species unique to the Kaibab. Major Powell left his imprint in this area, too, calling it Kaibab after the Paiute Indians name *Kai-vav-wi*, which means "mountains lying down."

Major John Wesley Powell, who provided the Grand Canyon's name, also came up with the name Glen Canyon when expounding on ". . . the carved walls, royal arches, glens . . ." unfortunately covered over by the Colorado's rising waters in 1957 after the Glen Canyon Dam was built.

Down to the Bottom

If you really want to take a journey through time, you might hike, as we did, on the Nankoweap Trail from the North Rim to the Colorado River.

It took a full day to reach the bottom on that back-pack trip and water was scarce. Although we each carried a gallon and a half, we used it up by midafternoon. In many places along the steep, rigorous trail, we had to lower our packs down and over ledges. Along the way we passed Indian petroglyphs and rock formations. The hike was worth the effort, because once on the banks of the Colorado River, the fishing for rainbow trout was excellent. Exhausted and a bit blistered, we camped overnight on a sandy beach, and next morning we were out casting and catching five-pound

Whitewater Challenge.
Rafters today have the advantage of sturdy rubber crafts that can withstand enormous pressure. In 1869, John Wesley Powell, a one-armed Civil War veteran, and his party traveled the Colorado throughout the canyon in three wooden boats. They found the water "too thin to plow and too thick to drink."

Buddy Mays

POINTS OF INTEREST: Arizona Tour 7

Northeastern Arizona

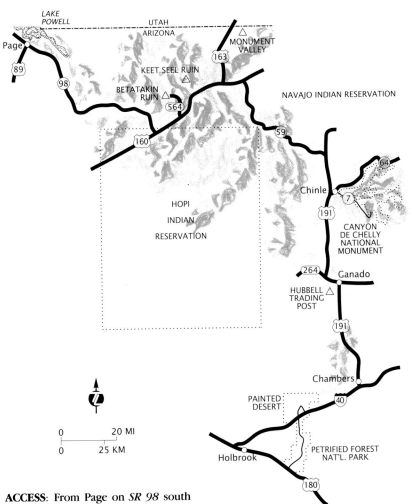

Buddy Mays

ACCESS: From Page on *SR 98* south *US 160*; *US 163* north to Monument Valley; *US 160* to *US 191* south to Canyon de Chelly; *I-40* east to Painted Desert and Petrified Forest.

INFORMATION: *Holbrook-Petrified Forest Chamber of Commerce*, 100 E. Arizona St., Holbrook 86025 (602) 524-6558.

ANNUAL EVENTS:

Holbrook: *Old Times Fiddlers' Contest, Navajo County Fair,* August; *Christmas Parade of Lights,* first Saturday in December.

MUSEUMS AND GALLERIES:

Navajo Indian Reservation: *Hubbell Trading Post National Historic Site,* Ganado (602) 755-3254, 55 miles northwest of Gallup, N.M. on SR 364, daily 8 A.M.–5 P.M. (to 6 P.M. in summer), except Thanksgiving, Christmas, and New Year's Day.

SPECIAL ATTRACTIONS:

Canyon de Chelly National Monument, (602) 674-5436, P.O. Box 588, Chinle 86503 (reservations for tours from Thunderbird Lodge, Box 548, Chinle 86503; (602) 674-5841/5842); *Monument Valley Navajo Tribal Park,* P.O. Box 93, Monument Valley, UT 84536, (801) 727-3287.

Page numbers in **boldface** refer to illustrations in the text.

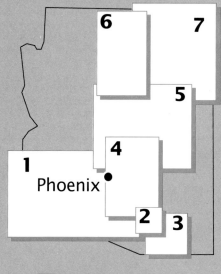

Tours